In the Vineyard
of the Lord

BY *Helen Steiner Rice*

In the Vineyard of the Lord

Helen Steiner Rice

as told to Fred Bauer

Guideposts
Carmel, New York 10512

Scripture quotations in this volume are from the King James Version of the Bible.

Excerpt from "Side By Side" by Harry Woods is Copyright MCMXXVII. Renewed by Shapiro, Bernstein & Co., Inc., New York, N.Y. 10022. Used by permission.

Illustrations by John Okladek

Library of Congress Cataloging in Publication Data

Rice, Helen Steiner.
  In the vineyard of the Lord.

  1. Rice,   Helen   Steiner—Biography. 2. Poets,   American—20th   century—
Biography. 3. Christian biography—United States. I. Bauer, Fred, fl. 1968-
  II. Title.
PS3568.I28Z467   811'.5'4 [B]   79-16686   ISBN 0-8007-1036-3

This Guideposts edition is published by
special arrangement with Fleming H. Revell Company.

Contents

Preface

Show me the way not to fortune or fame,
Not how to win laurels or praise for my name—
But show me the way to spread the Great Story
That "Thine is The Kingdom and Power and Glory."

Nothing I have ever written so clearly expresses my philosophy as the prayer-poem above. Fame and fortune are not my goals, nor have they ever been. That is because I learned very early in life that the praise of fellowmen and women—though pleasant and gratifying—was a transitory and fickle thing. And because it is no more lasting than the seafoam which rides a wave to shore, I searched for and found something in life that *is* eternal. It is God's unending love, which is able to sustain all of us through any reversal life sends our way.

Because my focus has been on God, I've never worried about the popularity of the verses I've written, or how widely known my name is. I have no great talent or unusual gift. I see myself as simply another worker in the vineyard of the Lord—one who seeks to do His will and point others to His eternal truths.

When my simple poems gained worldwide exposure, I was amazed but not overwhelmed. For some reason, known to God, He had a purpose for them and a mission for me; I accept what has happened, not as a personal accomplishment or triumph, but as another example of His miraculous power. He is the inspiration; I am only an instrument, repeating in rhyme the words of faith and hope He has placed on my heart.

So when people write, phone, or cable me from great distances, saying that they want to come and meet me, I try to discourage them. What you read in my poems is all I have to say. My genealogy is undistinguished. I am no celebrity or rare talent. In verse I tell them:

People everywhere in life
    from every walk and station,
From every town and city
    and every state and nation

> Have given me so many things
> intangible and dear,
> I couldn't begin to count them all
> or even make them clear . . .
> I only know I owe so much
> to people everywhere
> And when I put my thoughts in verse
> it's just a way to share
> The musings of a thankful heart
> a heart much like your own,
> For nothing that I think or write
> is mine and mine alone . . .
> So if you found some beauty
> in any word or line,
> It's just "Your Soul's Reflection
> in Proximity with Mine."

Or, as I wrote in another disclaimer to those who were trying to mantle me with great wisdom and new truth:

> We all need words to live by,
> To inspire us and guide us,
> Words to give us courage
> When the trials of life betide us—
> And the words that never fail us—
> Are the words of God above,
> Words of comfort and of courage
> Filled with wisdom and with love—
> They are ageless and enduring,
> They have lived through generations,
> There's no question left unanswered
> In our Father's revelations—
> And in this ever-changing world
> God's words remain unchanged,
> For though through countless ages
> They've been often re-arranged,
> The TRUTH shines through all changes
> Just as BRIGHT TODAY as WHEN
> OUR FATHER MADE THE UNIVERSE
> And breathed His Life in men—
> And the words of inspiration
> That I write for you today
> Are just the old enduring truths

Said in a rhythmic way—
And if my "borrowed words of truth"
In some way touch your heart,
Then I am deeply thankful
To have had a little part
In sharing these GOD-GIVEN LINES,
And I hope you'll share them, too,
With family, friends and loved ones
And all those dear to YOU.

So you can understand why I have resisted publishers who have come to me asking that I write my life story. "Who would be interested?" I ask. "Thousands," I have been told. To which I respond, then, that people are too interested in who we are and not interested enough in what each of us can be through God's Holy Spirit. It is our Heavenly Father who holds the key to deeper life and deeper understanding, not people. They, at best, can only be reflections of His perfection, copies of the genuine article.

But publishers are very persuasive. They insisted that my story could help others find the Source of Life and could inspire them in their walk of faith. If that were true, I said finally, I would try, provided my friend Fred Bauer would lend me an editorial hand. When he agreed to help, I agreed to write a "selective" autobiography, drawing upon incidents that center on God's goodness and steadfastness—not mine. My hope and prayer, then, is that this book will bring glory to God Almighty, the Maker and Sustainer of life, now and forevermore.

HELEN STEINER RICE

Part I:
The Early Years

1 Lorain, Ohio

LORD, SHOW ME THE WAY

Lord, show me the way
I can somehow repay
The blessings You've given to me . . .
Lord, teach me to do
What You most want me to
And to be what You want me to be . . .
I'm unworthy I know
But I do love You so—
I beg You to answer my plea . . .
I've not much to give
But as long as I live
May I give it completely to Thee!

*L*ife, it has been said, is divided into seven ages—infancy, childhood, adolescence, young adulthood, early middle age, later middle life, and old age. But I see the seventy-nine years God has given me not in seven segments but in three. The first two cover approximately thirty years each; the last, still incomplete, has covered nineteen.

Breaking those three divisions down, the first was from birth till my husband's death in 1931. The second segment went from the time I came to Cincinnati and joined the Gibson Greeting Company, until one of my poems was presented over television on the "Lawrence Welk Show" in 1960. And the third period covers the years since—the most hectic years—exciting years—trying years—blessed years.

So, taking the first of those three periods in chronological order, let me tell you a little about my early life—first, my growing-up years. I was born May 19, 1900 in the lakefront city of Lorain, Ohio, about thirty miles west of Cleveland. I say "city" with the footnote that my birthplace had gained that distinction only four years earlier, in 1896. An iron and steel center, it was an industrial place, bustling with commercial activity. Lorain's fine harbor made it a heavily trafficked freighter port for incoming iron and coal, and the community was served by several railroads—the New York Central, the Nickle Plate, the Lorain & West Virginia, and the Baltimore & Ohio among them.

13

Of course, my earliest memories have nothing to do with commerce or business or history, but with my mother and father, my younger sister, Gertrude, my friends, and neighbors.

Lorain was a charming, friendly place, a secure place, an idyllic place. Clean as a hound's tooth, it was a community for people who took a great deal of pride in their families, churches, homes, streets, and yards. When I think back to those times when neighbors were neighborly, people were caring and helpful, kind and generous, I find it hard to believe what has happened to some of our cities. In their bigness and anonymity, many have become jungles of depravity and bigotry and crime—dirty and uncivilized.

My longing for those earlier, simpler, more gracious times once prompted me to write a poem called "Heart Gifts."

It's not the things that can be bought
that are life's richest treasure,
It's just the little
"heart gifts"
that money cannot measure. . .
A cheerful smile, a friendly word,
a sympathetic nod
Are priceless little treasures
from the storehouse
of our God . . .
They are the things that can't be bought
with silver or with gold,
For thoughtfulness and kindness
and love are never sold . . .
They are the priceless things in life
for which no one can pay,
And the giver finds rich recompense
In Giving Them Away.

2 *My Family*

GOD'S LOVE IS FOREVER

The Seasons swiftly come and go
And with them comes the thought
Of all the various changes
That time in flight has brought . . .
But one thing never changes,
It remains the same forever,
God truly loves His children
And He will forsake them never.

Mark Twain once wrote: "In Boston they ask, 'How much does he know?' In New York, 'How much is he worth?' In Philadelphia, 'Who were his parents?' "

None of the three questions has ever been of much interest to me when it comes to people. So when admirers of my verse write to ask me personal questions about my family background, I am not very expansive, and with good cause. I simply don't know much about my roots. It's not very important in God's eyes—man's financial worth, his knowledge or his parentage—so why should it be in ours? The primary question we need to answer is, "How are we using the life God gave us?" If we are engaged in living for His glory and the good of others around us, then our lives speak well of us and do honor to our forebears. Having made that point, let me say that I was blessed with hardy, healthy, honest, hardworking ancestors.

My mother, Anna Bieri, was born of first-generation parents who immigrated here in the late 1800s from Bern, Switzerland. They settled on a small farm near Wooster, Ohio. The land there was not the best, so the Bieris had to struggle to make a living, something that soured my mother on farm life forever. When her sister married an artist and moved to Cleveland, she vowed to follow, and she did as soon as she had finished high school.

My father, John A. Steiner, was born of German stock, his parents owning a very successful dairy farm near Sterling, Ohio, not far from Wooster. The Steiners' cattle were some of the finest around, and I am told that their well-painted house and barns drew approving comments from all who rode past in their horse-drawn buggies.

Of all my grandparents, only Grandma Bieri has a special place in my memory. That is because she lived with our family in Lorain from time to time. After her husband died, she moved from child to child, staying with one for a while, then another.

What a dear woman she was, a real old-fashioned grandma. Stooped and wearied from all her years of hard work on the farm, she still had a wonderful spirit and a deep Christian faith. She also had a big lap on which I sat at every opportunity. When she was staying with us, I'd make a beeline for her room after school and excitedly tell her of the day's happenings. She listened with the full attention only grandmas have time to give. Always, I'd find her bent over her large German Bible, which rested on a stand near the window. She studied God's Word by the hour. Not good with the English language, even after a lifetime in America, Grandma Bieri got by with a few words of approval, a wonderfully accepting smile and a love that was irrepressible.

On Sunday nights, we'd have our family worship time. That was one of the blessings of a radioless, televisionless era: there was time for family conversation. Without fail, I'd climb up on a chair and preach, using all the Bible verses I knew. This pleased my grandma greatly, and with adoring eyes she would tell Mother in German, "How that girl can preach!"

One of the saddest times in my early childhood came when Grandma fell and hurt herself. My sister, Gertrude, and I were out walking with her in the nearby woods. When we tried to cross a stream that ran through them, Grandma Bieri slipped and broke her arm.

I cried a prayer that night that God would heal her quickly—which in time He did. Grandma tried only to minimize her discomfort, embarrassed that she'd caused so much commotion. She was always afraid that she would impose on our family and be a nuisance. Her selflessness was an inspiration to all and a testimony to the faith she held so close. Without fail, she was always concerned about others.

3 My Father

FATHERS ARE WONDERFUL PEOPLE

Fathers are wonderful people
      too little understood,
And we do not sing their praises
      as often as we should . . .
For, somehow, Father seems to be
      the man who pays the bills,
While Mother binds up little hurts
      and nurses all our ills . . .
And Father struggles daily
      to live up to *"his image"*
As protector and provider
      and "hero of the scrimmage" . . .
And perhaps that is the reason
      we sometimes get the notion
That Fathers are not subject
      to the thing we call emotion,
But if you look inside Dad's heart,
      where no one else can see,
You'll find he's sentimental
      and as "soft" as he can be . . .
But he's so busy every day
      in the grueling race of life,
He leaves the sentimental stuff
      to his partner and his wife . . .
But Fathers are just *wonderful*
      in a million different ways,
And they merit loving compliments
      and accolades of praise,
For the only reason Dad aspires
      to fortune and success
Is to make the family proud of him
      and to bring them happiness . . .
And like *Our Heavenly Father,*
      he's a guardian and a guide,
Someone that we can count on
      to be *always on our side.*

*T*he kindness my father showed Grandma Bieri is probably one of the best ways to characterize his gentle, caring nature. Some men would have resented the presence of a mother-in-law in their home, but Dad went out of his way to make her feel welcome and comfortable. And she loved him like a son.

As I told you earlier, Dad grew up on a dairy farm where he learned the discipline of hard work. But he also learned to love the outdoors and nature, and have an appreciation of it. He worked hard and he played hard.

Big and strong, he was an avid fisherman and hunter from his boyhood, and he never lost his love for these outdoor pastimes—much to the annoyance of Mother, who thought them folly. When hunting season came, he was not above laying off work to take some of his friends afield. (And his friends included people from all strata of the community—bankers, doctors, lawyers, ministers, field hands, the rich, the poor, educated, and not.)

"If you have too much time of your hands, John," I once heard my mother say in the midst of hunting season, "I've got several chores for you around the house."

"Well, if it's housework you have for me," he answered good-naturedly, "I might as well go back to the railroad."

Dad was an engineer on the Baltimore & Ohio railroad all of his married life. That was part of the wedding contract. Mother so despised the hard life of the farm that she vowed she would never marry a farmer, which is why Dad eventually changed vocations. He'd been smitten by this Wooster beauty while still helping on the family farm, but her ultimatum about not marrying a farmer led to his defection from rural life.

In addition to the farm, the Steiners also owned a restaurant, which was at a railroad crossroads. One day, talking with a group of railroaders who had stopped by for lunch, Dad inquired about jobs on the railroad. He was especially interested in becoming an engineer. They told him he'd first have to become a fireman. Because he was so well liked by everyone who ever knew him, he had no trouble finding a sponsor to recommend him for a job on the Baltimore & Ohio, and with that move he clinched Anna Bieri's heart and hand.

My memories of my father are all good ones. Never in my life did he spank me; never was he anything but loving and caring.

4 *My Mother*

A MOTHER'S LOVE

A Mother's love is something
      that no one can explain,
It is made of deep devotion
      and of sacrifice and pain,
It is endless and unselfish
      and enduring come what may
For nothing can destroy it
      or take that love away . . .
It is patient and forgiving
      when all others are forsaking,
And it never fails or falters
      even though the heart is breaking . . .
It believes beyond believing
      when the world around condemns,
And it glows with all the beauty
      of the rarest, brightest gems . . .
It is far beyond defining,
      it defies all explanation,
And it still remains a secret
      like the mysteries of creation . . .
A many-splendored miracle
      man cannot understand
And another wondrous evidence
      of God's tender guiding hand.

*I*n addition to an adorably kind and considerate father, I was blessed with a loving mother who made me feel like the most special girl in the world.

A short woman of petite build, she had the beauty and poise and personality to light up any room she entered. Though born into a poor farm family, she was committed to making something of herself; as soon as she was old enough, she followed her married sister to Cleveland. There she found work in what was called a "sewing room"—a business establishment that catered to the wealthier women of that city. More than a fine seamstress, Mother had a creative flair in colorful clothing that soon turned her into a much-sought-after designer.

Marriage slowed that career, even though she continued to make clothing for some clients who followed her out to Lorain. I cannot recall seeing any of her early handiwork, except for her wedding trousseau, which was gorgeous. From time to time when I needed a dress for some special occasion, Mother would draw from her wardrobe a creation which she would cut down and refashion for me. I can still see the excitement in her eyes when she was sewing something new for me. Making stylish clothing was her unique talent, and she was most fulfilled when she was at work at her calling.

Mother thought one always should look his or her best. She would not go outside the house without arranging her hair, "putting on her face," and carefully choosing her dress, and she insisted that Gertie and I take the same pains with our appearance. I was a willing follower; Gertie resisted. She was too busy with her young friends to worry about vanity.

Once when Easter neared, Mother took us to Mrs. Storey's, the town's finest milliner. First she outfitted me with a new dress and new hat, carefully selecting the prettiest ones available. I was in seventh heaven, ogling one fashion, then another. When Mother and I had decided on my Easter finery, she turned her attention on a reluctant Gertie, who must have been five or six years old. One dress in particular seemed to be made for my sister, but she hated it. Taking hold of the blue ribbon that decorated the bodice, she gave it a pull and separated it from the dress.

"We'll take it," Mother responded quickly, much to Mrs. Storey's relief, I'm sure. Then Mother sought a suitable hat. One after another, she placed hats on my bored sister's head. When none seemed to please, Mother decided for her.

"I think this red chiffon one is perfect," she said, placing it again on Gertie's tilted head. Her curls bloused out beneath it, giving her an angelic appearance.

"Oh, it's . . . it's heavenly," I prompted.

Whereupon, Gertie stuck out her tongue at me and threw the hat across the room, like a red chiffon Frisbee. "Oh," Mother said in disgust, "why can't you be like Helen?"

So on Easter Sunday, when we paraded from our Lexington Avenue house to the Twentieth Street Methodist Church, Mother and I were dressed to the nines, while Gertie trailed along, hatless and in a ribbonless dress. I've never seen a red hat since but what I've thought of Gertie's toss in Mrs. Storey's Millinery Shop. It was no doubt a first—and a last.

It was a few more years before I understood that Easter was more than new dresses and new hats. Later, I put that understanding to verse . . .

> In the glorious Easter Story
> A troubled world can find
> Blessed reassurance
> And enduring peace of mind . . .
> For though we grow discouraged
> In this world we're living in,
> There is comfort just in knowing
> God has triumphed over sin . . .
> For our Saviour's Resurrection
> Was God's way to telling men
> That in Christ we are eternal
> And in Him we live again . . .
> And to know life is unending
> And God's love is unending, too,
> Makes our daily tasks and burdens
> So much easier to do . . .
> For the blessed Easter Story
> Of Christ the living Lord,
> Makes our earthly sorrow nothing
> When compared with this reward.

The Glory of the Easter Story

5 Growing Up

A CHILD'S FAITH

"Jesus loves me, this I know,
For the BIBLE tells me so"—
Little children ask no more,
For love is all they're looking for,
And in a small child's shining eyes
The FAITH of all the ages lies—
And tiny hands and tousled heads
That kneel in prayer by little beds
Are closer to the dear Lord's heart
And of His Kingdom more a part
Than we who search, and never find,
The answers to our questioning mind
For FAITH in things we cannot see
Requires a child's simplicity
For, lost in life's complexities,
We drift upon uncharted seas
And slowly FAITH disintegrates
While wealth and power accumulates—
And the more man learns, the less he knows,
And the more involved his thinking grows
And, in his arrogance and pride,
No longer is man satisfied
To place his confidence and love
With childlike FAITH in God above—
Oh, Father, grant once more to men
A simple childlike FAITH again
And, with a small child's trusting eyes,
May all men come to realize
That FAITH alone can save man's soul
And lead him to a HIGHER GOAL.

*N*o one could have had a happier, more secure childhood than I. My early years were complete in every sense of the word.

These years were normal ones with one exception. I must have been very precocious and was inclined to seek the companionship of adults rather than children my own age. I think it was their conversation and ideas that fascinated me. For that reason, I was always more comfortable and happier to be around older people.

That is not to say I didn't engage in normal activities for people my age. I had my dolls, and Mother helped me make attractive clothes for them (naturally!), and I was active in school programs and anything that transpired at church. But the adult world was magnetic, and I was most anxious to be a part of it.

One adult I remember in particular was Mr. Campbell, who lived across the street from us. He was a salesman for *Encyclopaedia Britannica,* and, being childless, he and his wife were only too happy to have me come visit them—which I did almost daily. The words and pictures in Mr. Campbell's latest edition of his line of books intrigued me immensely, and my thirst for the information in them was fathomless. After Mr. Campbell was finished with one year's edition, he'd give me his old sample, which I treasured and reread again and again.

When I insisted on going over to the Campbells' to read one day in deference to playing, Gertrude waved me off with a scornful "you and your dictionaries!" Little did I know that words and the images they created were to become the focus of my life.

For the most part I was a healthy child with only minor illnesses. Once I do remember being confined to bed with a burning fever and the all-night vigil of my parents who bathed me with cool cloths to keep my temperature down. Hearing my father's quiet voice at my bedside through long dark hours was particularly comforting. For a big man—he was over six-foot-three—he had the most reassuringly quiet voice I've ever heard. He would have made a great doctor.

Only in the last few years—in my seventies—have I known deep pain, the kind that makes one sometimes long for his or her heavenly home. When a friend heard me remark that I was ready to go and be with my Heavenly Father, she replied "Oh, no, Helen, the world would be denied the comfort of the verses still inside you."

I told her I had written most of the things God had laid on my heart. Furthermore, if He took me He would find another to carry on. He always has. None of us is indispensable. Yet, I believe that God has a plan for each of our lives and that if we allow Him, He will see that plan to completion. The Bible verses in Matthew 10:29, 30 tell us that every hair on our heads is numbered and that not a sparrow falls without the knowledge of our Heavenly Father. So when we fret about this or that happening, we do so in vain. God directs the universe and He guides the lives of all His children who are obedient and willing to give Him charge.

My faith seemingly has been a part of me for as long as I can remember. Of course, my mother and Grandma Bieri were devoted Christians and their examples were important. Also, my early training at the Twentieth Street Methodist Church was a faith builder.

We attended church every Sunday without fail. After Sunday school, most of the children were allowed to leave, but on many occasions I was asked to stay and recite some Scripture we'd learned. "Won't you say the Twenty-third Psalm for the worship service, Helen?" the minister asked one Sunday. When I answered that I'd be happy to do it, Gertrude became instantly sick to her stomach.

"Yuck," she said (or words to that effect) about my willingness to please adults.

Before I was out of elementary school, I was teaching a Sunday-school class myself. Several years later, looking at a picture of my class, I realized that I was not much older than my pupils. As I said, I was anxious to become an adult.

My high-school years were crammed with busyness as I participated in all the activities a day would hold. One discovery was an interest and skill in public speaking. Another was a love for poetry. On more than one occasion I tried my hand at writing verses, as these two examples from the school newspaper show:

APRIL

April comes with cheeks a-glowing,
Silver streams are all a-flowing,
Flowers open wide their eyes
In a rapturous surprise.
Lilies dream beside the brooks,
Violets in meadow nooks,
And the birds gone wild with glee,
Fill the woods with melody.

Winds are soft and fields are fair,
Blue the sky and sweet the air.
And the happy, blushing earth
Laughs at every flower's birth.
Golden days and silver nights,
Hours brim with calm delights,
Lilies chime and blue bells ring,
"Welcome, welcome to the Spring!"

1916, *The Scimitar*,
Lorain High School

WEAVER OF DREAMS

Weaver of dreams, come near I pray,
Weave me a scene of childhood's day,
Weave it slowly with touch so true,
Weave it in every brightest hue.
Weave it in colors blue and gold,
Weave it in outline clear and bold,
Weave it in love and youthful joys,
Weave it in happy girls and boys.
Weave me scenes of the house next door,
Weave me pictures of those I adore,
Weave me scenes of childhood's bliss,
Weave me the thrills of childhood's kiss,
Weave me scenes of a towering school,
Weave it supreme in its glorious rule,
Weave me pictures of teachers kind,
Weave me all these ties that bind.

Weaver of dreams with magic thread,
Weave me the joys of a day that's dead
Then may I drift over peaceful seasons,
Back through your web of memories.

1917, *The Scimitar*, Lorain High School

By the time May 1918 and graduation arrived, I had made up my mind that I wanted to be a lawyer. With the exception of algebra (which I loathed because of the teacher), I got straight A's and graduated with honors.

A news item about me in the Lorain paper announced with a substantial headline that a Lorain girl was planning to study law. The emphasis was on the word *girl*. I had never let my sex deter me from any goal and I was sure it wouldn't make me any less effective as a lawyer; but I was not anticipating a family tragedy that lay just over the horizon—one that would give my life a new direction.

6 *The 1918 Epidemic*

THE END OF THE ROAD
IS BUT A BEND IN THE ROAD

When we feel we have nothing left to give
And we are sure that the "song has ended"—
When our day seems over and the shadows fall
And the darkness of night has descended,
Where can we go to find the strength
To valiantly keep on trying,
Where can we find the hand that will dry
The tears that the heart is crying—
There's but one place to go and that is to God
And, dropping all pretense and pride,
We can pour out our problems without restraint
And gain strength with Him at our side—
And together we stand at life's crossroads
And view what we think is the end,
But God has a much bigger vision
And He tells us it's ONLY A BEND—
For the road goes on and is smoother,
And the "pause in the song" is a "rest,"
And the part that's unsung and unfinished
Is the sweetest and richest and best—
So rest and relax and grow stronger,
LET GO and LET GOD share your load,
Your work is not finished or ended,
You've just come to "A BEND IN THE ROAD."

*I*n early life, most of us are spared most of living's toughest realities. Accidents and tragedies, major setbacks and defeats, illness and death are things we believe happen to people other than ourselves. But the longer we live, the more we come to realize that dark clouds are as much a part of living as sunshine, and no one is forever free of pain and trouble and affliction.

Of course, without night we'd never come to appreciate day, and without obstacles we'd never be able to fully realize how magnificent are the many gifts and blessings of life bestowed upon us by God.

Against a backdrop of deep parental love with all its support and security came an experience in my eighteenth year that was to alter not only my understanding of life's fragility, but was to dramatically change the very course of my life.

In June of 1918 while the country's focus was on Europe and the "war that would end all wars," I was blithely looking forward to college. Then, the devastating worldwide influenza epidemic struck, delivering a blow that touched just about every American family in one way or another. If an immediate family member was not stricken, then more than likely a relative or friend was afflicted.

Most recovered, but many died—some 20 million around the world, more than half a million in this country. The latter figure is even more shocking when one considers that America only had about 100 million citizens at that time.

The Steiners were not spared. On a train run from Cleveland to Chicago, my father became ill and was unable to work the return trip. They brought him home and he was put to bed. Though we were concerned, I was sure he'd be well in a matter of days. I could not conceive of a world without him. Big and strong and in his early forties, he would recover; I knew it. But when Mother told us how serious his condition was, we went to our knees in prayer like never before.

"Lord, please make Daddy well," I pleaded. "He's such a good man and we need him so much." But his condition worsened. Mother called his sister in from Sterling to help care for him. Then the doctor came one morning, gave him medicine, and advised Mother that he was sinking. By that afternoon his breathing had grown more labored and his temperature had climbed. The doctor returned before dinner, then emerging from the bedroom said

"I'm sorry, but he's gone." Then he hurriedly excused himself. There were so many others who needed him—so many others who were losing loved ones.

The great emptiness I felt that lonely night still causes something to stir inside me. I was so young, so naïve, so vulnerable, so unaccepting. In a few days my beloved father had been taken from Mother, Gertrude and me. It was unjust, cruel, unexplainable.

I remember standing alone, the night Dad died, on the back steps of our Reid Avenue house, crying into the dark night, "Why, God, why?"

But I could hear no answer.

7 *To Work*

ON THE WINGS OF PRAYER

Just close your eyes and open your heart
And feel your worries and cares depart,
Just yield yourself to the Father above
And let Him hold you secure in HIS love—

*T*he loss of the family breadwinner necessitated some changes. Though we weren't destitute, I am sure Mother was concerned about our future. Still, she didn't burden her children with her anxieties, and with the help of insurance and a pension we managed. A few adjustments were required, and my college education was something I decided to forego.

Mother—always the optimist, a person who believed that where there was a will, there was a way—insisted that I go to Ohio State as planned. "We'll find the money," she said. But I knew that she needed Gertrude and me, and I decided to go to work.

"Maybe I'll go to college next year," I told her. But next year never came and I got my education another way. "Where are you going to look for a job?" Gertie asked.

"I don't know," I said. "Maybe something will turn up."

Then something amazing happened. Before I could even apply anywhere for a job, someone called me and offered me one. This phenomenon has repeated itself several times since. Surprising though it may seem, I have never applied for a job in my life, and with one short exception, I have supported myself since I was eighteen.

I believe there is a spiritual principle involved, one that is alluded to in Isaiah 65:24. It reads, ". . . before they call, I will answer; and while they are yet speaking, I will hear."

As I have made prayer a regular part of my life, a daily, hourly, moment-by-moment demonstration of my faith, I have had an open line with my Heavenly Father, and He has been aware of my needs before I've petitioned Him. I don't mean that I've been one to walk around with my hands folded in constant prayer and my eyes heavenward. No—not that kind of devotion—but the kind that recognizes dependence upon God for everything. I am from the same school as the saint who advised,

"Pray as if everything depended upon God, and work as if everything depended upon you."

Whatever, before I filled out my first resume or knocked on my first door, Mr. Quillin of the Electric Light and Power Company of Lorain called and asked if I'd come downtown to his office and talk about working there.

I had no idea what job he had in mind, but the next day I showed up and he asked me if I'd like to learn to make silk lampshades. "I don't know," I answered. "How did you choose me for this assignment?"

"I called the high-school home-economics department," he answered, "and your teacher said you had a flair for clothing and decoration."

He went on to explain that the light-fixture business was booming in the East, and he was sure women in Lorain would be caught up in the movement, if he had someone who was a trained interior decorator who could show them how to make beautiful lampshades to decorate their homes. Of course, the light company wasn't interested in interior decoration. They wanted to sell appliances, which would increase the consumption of electricity. (Oh, how times change!)

"We'll pay you and cover all your expenses if you'll go to Cleveland for three months to learn the business," Mr. Quillin said. When I heard the salary, I agreed.

While I was being taught the art of making lampshades, Mr. Quillin was busy importing exquisite silks of every imaginable color, as well as attractive bases for the light fixtures. When I completed my training, I was given a prominent place in the store, near the front door and near a window. Everyone who entered and everyone who passed by could see me working on my creations. The fad caught on, and women by the score were crowded around me for months, learning how to create their own lampshades. I don't know how much additional electricity was sold, but I know Mr. Quillin was very enthusiastic about my contribution.

My satisfaction was in helping maintain our family. Though the loss of my father was to have a great influence on the direction of our lives, the fact that we were able to continue to get along gave Mother, Gertrude, and me great satisfaction, and it established a bond that was to grow deeper as a result.

8 A Prizewinner

GOD BLESS AMERICA

"AMERICA THE BEAUTIFUL"—
May it always stay that way—
But to keep "OLD GLORY" flying
There's a price that we must pay . . .
For everything worth having
Demands work and sacrifice,
And FREEDOM is a GIFT from God
That commands the HIGHEST PRICE . . .
For all our wealth and progress
Are worthless as can be
Without the FAITH that made us great
And kept OUR COUNTRY FREE . . . .

For more than two years I helped hundreds, no, thousands of Lorain women make silk lampshades for their homes. The company was pleased that so many responded, and I was pleased to be able to help so many homemakers create something beautiful for their houses at a fraction of the cost of store-bought shades.

But at that point I was ready to move on to something else. One day I read about a window-decorating contest sponsored by the Sunny Suds Washing Machine Company. I asked Mr. Quillin if I could decorate a window, and he agreed to let me try, after he learned that it could be done without great expense and on my own time.

As an added feature to the display (which was designed to encourage giving washing machines for Christmas), I wrote a poem about how happy Mom would be all year long if she received a Sunny Suds washer.

'Cause Santa, old dear,
In his wisdom so great,
Took care of us all
On this lucky old date,
For he placed near the tree
A Sunny Suds bright
And Mother is happy,
For to wash is delight.

The window proved to be quite a conversation piece, resulted in increased sales, and made me a prizewinner. For my efforts, I received a thirty-dollar check. From that point forward, I was put in charge of trimming all the windows, and that led to writing the company's newspaper advertisements, and eventually to direct selling.

When I was given responsibility for all floor sales, I was soon hailed in the company newsletter as the top salesperson with an average of three thousand dollars in sales a month—which at that time represented a lot of washers, sweepers, stoves, heaters, toasters, and so on.

Selling always has fascinated me—not from the standpoint of foisting merchandise upon people who have no need for it, but from the standpoint of helping people make wise purchasing decisions. Over the years, I've come to have a great appreciation and admiration of men and women in sales. The good ones love their work and are the very backbone of any successful company.

Upon occasion, I was asked to put my advertising and sales psychology into articles for various company publications. Not long ago, an ancient clipping of an article I'd done for the Hoover sweeper people surfaced from the back of my files. In it I said that rhyme could be an effective attention-getting device for ad or window display, and proceeded to share one I'd used to hawk sweepers:

> Your room shines out in splendor,
> No dirt or dust is seen,
> Because the rugs within your house
> Are bright and Hoover-clean.

Over the next couple of years, I won several more prizes for advertising and sales, but it was a 1924 contest sponsored by *Forbes* magazine which proved to be a career changer. Writing on the subject "How Sound Public Relations Can Be Developed and Maintained," I received a special award and a trip to Atlantic City for the presentation. In addition to my work for the light company, I had been writing and publishing some greeting-card verse for the Midwest Publishing Company, and doing some public speaking around the state. But when I won the *Forbes* prize, speaking opportunities flooded in.

One of the offers I accepted the following year took me to Washington, D.C., where I spoke to a national gathering of electrical railway officials. As was often the case then, I was the only woman on the program. Afterward, one of the officers asked me if I'd like to accompany a group which had been invited to the White House. What twenty-five-year-old would refuse *that* opportunity? When it came time to take the customary news photo, I—being the only female present—was told to stand next to

President Coolidge. When the picture appeared in hundreds of newspapers across the country, the interest in the "businesswoman from Lorain, Ohio" opened even more doors. Before I knew it, I was in demand as a speaker from coast to coast. "Only in America," someone said, and it is true—we live in a land of great opportunity.

9 *Public Speaker*

OPEN MY EYES

God open my eyes
        so I may see
And feel Your presence
        close to me . . .
Give me strength
        for my stumbling feet
As I battle the crowd
        on life's busy street,
And widen the vision
        of my unseeing eyes
So in passing faces
        I'll recognize
Not just a stranger,
        unloved and unknown,
But a friend with a heart
        that is much like my own . . .
Give me perception
        to make me aware
That scattered profusely
        on life's thoroughfare
Are the best GIFTS of GOD
        that we daily pass by
As we look at the world
        with an UNSEEING EYE

The setting was the waiting room of a small railroad station, where three women huddled together on the tall wooden benches provided for train passengers.

One, the mother of the other two, was giving last minute instructions to the older of her two daughters, who was about to leave on a train. "Now don't be afraid to ask for help when you get to Chicago," the mother said.

The woman of twenty-five nodded solicitously. Then the whistle of the approaching train brought them outside where bags were loaded, good-byes said, kisses and waves exchanged to the sound of the steam engine.

The Chicago-bound woman in the picture was me—off on my first long-distance speaking date. It was to become commonplace, my dashing all over the country to give lectures, but as with all new adventures, my stomach was full of butterflies that day.

New undertakings have a way of instilling most people with fear—fear that they will fail, or show their ignorance, or make fools of themselves—but the Chicago date went well and it served as a confidence-builder for what was to follow.

Because I have always enjoyed meeting people, and because I care about them, my evolution from public-utilities employee to full-time public speaker was a natural one. Forming my own lecture bureau, I drew on my background in public relations and advertising to tout Helen Steiner.

A faded pamphlet from an old scrapbook reveals that I was no shrinking violet when it came to self-promotion! *Write the Steiner Service for open dates*, the brochure advised. It also included quotes from satisfied clients.

> Miss Steiner drew the largest crowd in the history of our association, and they liked her immensely.
>
> ———
>
> In Ohio, they call Helen Steiner "The Lorain Tornado." After hearing her *powerful* speech, I know why.
>
> ———
>
> Known coast to coast as "The Sweetheart of the Electrical Industry," her wit, charm and knowledge make her a delightful speaker.
>
> ———
>
> The meeting broke into cheers for Helen Steiner several times. Part of her talk was done in rhyme, and her remarks delighted the audience.
>
> ———
>
> She is peppy and knows her subject, and she landed with both feet, high heels and all, right into the midst of the good graces of her audience.
>
> ———

The advertising flier also included my subjects, some of which were "Living and Working Enthusiastically"; "Do You Know Your Business or Do You Love It?"; "The Man May Pay, But It's the Woman Who Buys"; and "Blue Eyes or Gray Matter?"

The latter was presented before scores of largely male audiences, urging men in management positions to wise up in their practices of hiring and promoting women.

"The more you expect of women," I told them, "the more they will accomplish, and the more your companies will benefit. There is nothing wrong with pretty blue eyes in business, if there is gray matter behind them."

Some have suggested I was fifty years ahead of my time—a feminist of the twenties. I don't know about that; I just saw bright women being overlooked because of their sex, and I thought it was terribly stupid and wasteful. The difference between myself and some others was probably my willingness to stand up and say it. Of course, women were coming into their own then. Susan B. Anthony didn't get the Nineteenth Amendment to the Bill of Rights ratified in 1920 without the support of millions of women.

In addition to speaking about women and their potential, I wrote articles for national publications, pointing out the business prudence of giving them equal opportunity. My tack was to show the dollars-and-cents wisdom of my position rather than to dwell on the injustice of prejudice. Hardheaded businessmen haven't changed. They talked about profit-and-loss statements then and like today they, too, wanted to know what the bottom line was. I told them women could help them improve their operations—and their images, too.

Women employees have the power within them to create goodwill for your company, I wrote once. Then I listed nine attributes which, in general, are still true. I think women are *ambitious, industrious, patient, dependable, friendly, adaptable, tactful, cheerful* and *neat.* I should have added *intuitive.* Over and over again, I have seen women in business draw on intuition to make a tough decision, and more often than not, their instincts proved correct.

As one would guess, I had some interesting experiences while I was on the lecture circuit. One engagement took me to Buffalo for a speech before a large audience of men. When I arrived at the hall, hundreds of men stood around smoking and talking, waiting for the luncheon. Lost in this sea of humanity, I finally in desperation asked a man if he could direct me to Mr. Storrer, my host.

"I'm sorry, ma'am," the concerned gentleman said as he craned his neck, searching the crowd, "but he's looking for our speaker—and so am I."

"Well, you can stop looking," I told him. "I'm Miss Steiner."

"You . . . *you?*" he stammered, looking at me dubiously. "Wait right here." A minute later, Mr. Storrer arrived on the scene—a tall, stern-looking man with broad shoulders and a stentorian voice.

"You are Miss Helen Steiner?" he said incredulously.

I nodded.

"There must be some mistake." Wearing one of my lavish hats (which had become a trademark) and outfitted in a fitted suit with a short skirt (which was fashionable at the time), I must have looked even younger than my twenty-five years.

Pulling myself up to my full five-feet-one-inch, I replied that I was indeed the speaker with whom they had contracted, and if he would lead me to the lectern, I would get on with my assignment.

"But . . . but this is a huge crowd that includes some of the leading business people of the city," he stammered. "Do you think you can make yourself heard?" (It was in a day before microphones were in wide use, but Mr. Storrer's *real* worry was that I wouldn't be able to hold their attention, and as a result he would be widely criticized for bringing in some harebrained girl.

Though his nervousness did nothing to bolster my confidence, I rose to the occasion and gave the gathering its money's worth. The newspaper used a picture of me on its front page and wrote in glowing superlatives about my speech. Mr. Storrer sent roses to my room, and a Chamber of Commerce committee insisted that I stay overnight to see the attractions of their city and visit Niagara Falls.

I'm glad I didn't disappoint Mr. Storrer—otherwise I have the feeling he may have jumped into the Falls!

10 A Date in Dayton

LOVE: GOD'S GIFT DIVINE

Love is enduring
And patient and kind,
It judges all things
With the heart not the mind,
And love can transform
The most commonplace
Into beauty and splendor
And sweetness and grace . . .
For love is unselfish,
Giving more than it takes,
And no matter what happens
Love never forsakes,
It's faithful and trusting
And always believing,
Guileless and honest
And never deceiving . . .
Yes, love is beyond
What man can define,
For love is immortal
And God's Gift is Divine!

For the next five years, I crisscrossed the country, espousing my views on women and work. A review in the *Denver Post* quoted me as saying, "Women are tired of being parsley on the platter of business." The *Cleveland Press:* "Women have foresworn the powder puff and have gotten down to business. It's bunk that all women only want a job until they can get married."

When one reporter asked me if I was shopping for a husband, I told him no. "But if in traveling around America I find a man I like well enough, believe me, I'm not going to hang onto a career—I'm going to marry him."

That statement was to prove prophetic. In June 1928, a speaking assignment took me to Dayton. More accurately, there were two speeches.

I was originally scheduled to speak only before the Dayton Clearing-house Association, an organization of bankers, at their annual dinner banquet; but when the Dayton Rotary Club learned I was coming, they invited me to speak to them at noon.

Before the second opportunity came along, I was thinking of trying to postpone the speaking date before the bankers until later. A friend of the family was getting married, and Gertrude wanted me to attend the wedding ceremony with her; but I decided I should keep my original commitment and accept the second one as well. It made a lucrative trip south, as I was getting two hundred dollars for banquets and one hundred dollars for luncheon dates, which was big money for speakers at that time. But what I didn't know was that the trip was to serve as an occasion for me to meet my future husband.

On the appointed date, June 27, 1928, I went to Dayton and spoke to the Rotarians at noon. Then I returned to the hotel to rest and get ready for my evening speech. I was speaking to them on the subject of "Do You Know Your Business or Do You Love It?"

At about 5:30, a man by the name of Franklin D. Rice arrived at the hotel to drive me to the country club, where the banquet was to be held. He was an engaging fellow, pleasant, personable, clean-cut, tall, with dark hair and brown eyes—though I'm sure none of these features made much of an impression on me then. I was too busy getting my thoughts together on the speech ahead. To be good at public speaking, one needs much concentration, and I gave my talks 100 percent. Also, I never ate before a speech, because food had a way of making me logy, and I discovered through trial and error that I was a sharper speaker, if I waited until after an engagement to eat.

The banquet was a success as was my speech. The bankers were in a good mood after a day of golf and a fine dinner, and they responded enthusiastically to my stories and remarks.

When the program finished, I was tired and more than ready to go back to the hotel, eat, take a bath, and go to sleep. My plans were to return to Lorain in the morning. On the way back to the hotel, however, Mr. Rice, my escort (who I learned was vice-president of Dayton Savings and Trust), asked if he could take me to dinner. I hesitated, but then agreed. We ate at a good restaurant and I enjoyed his conversation. Other than that I have no impressions of the evening. Oh, he did tell me when he returned me to the hotel, "I'll send you newspaper clippings—if there are any."

"My dear man," I said, without a modicum of modesty, "in most cities where I speak they give me front-page coverage!"

"Oh, I don't know much about these things," he answered meekly.

A few days later, Mr. Rice called to inquire if I'd be home that coming weekend. When I said I would, he told me he had some newspaper clippings. "And, Miss Steiner," he added, "you *were* on the front page."

That Sunday afternoon, a huge limousine rolled up in front of 2714 Reid Avenue in Lorain, and window curtains up and down the street were drawn back as neighbors took notice. The car was driven by a chauffeur with Franklin in the rear. He came inside, met Mother and Gertrude, and took me for a ride. It was the first of many visits, letters, and phone calls.

I was the talk of the town. "Where did you catch him?" friends wanted to know. "I didn't catch him anywhere because I haven't been fishing," I answered. And it was the truth. I didn't fall head over heels in love with him. It was a relationship that simply grew.

When he told me he had broken his engagement to Bernice Chrysler of the automotive family, I was surprised. I hadn't even known he was engaged.

Then, one day he called to say he was coming to Cleveland that weekend for a sail in his boat on the lake (Lake Erie). "I'm bringing my mother, and thought that maybe you, your mother, and sister would like to join us."

"Not me," said Mother. "These people are out of our class, and I think you'd better recognize that before you get hurt." I knew the Rices were extremely wealthy, but Franklin was a very down-to-earth person of whom I'd grown very fond. I told Mother I had no intention of ending a relationship because of something as superficial as money.

"I'm going with the Rices this weekend whether you want to go or not." Gertrude sided with me and joined in for a weekend of fun.

It wasn't long before Franklin asked me to marry him. I asked for time to think it over.

Meanwhile, he arranged for my family to go to Dayton for a Thanksgiving dinner to get acquainted with his people. By now Mother knew I was serious about Franklin, and she agreed to come.

The dinner was an elaborate affair, eight courses with gourmet fare and all kinds of delicacies served by uniformed servants. The memory that sticks in my mind are two remarks, one made by Franklin's brother, Elwood (who was an enormously wealthy New York City banker), and one made by Franklin's mother.

"I understand my brother wants to marry you," Elwood said, loud enough for all to hear. Then he pointedly added, "I doubt that you would ever feel at home with us, my dear." The implication was clear! I was out of my league with people of such high social standing.

Before I could respond, Franklin moved toward his brother, his face flushed—more angry than I'd ever seen him.

"I'll thank you to take care of your own life," he barked. "I'm quite capable of running my own."

Mother Rice led me to another room while tempers cooled. "Don't pay any attention to Elwood," she advised. "He is too class-conscious to suit any of us. I hope you'll marry Franklin. I knew he was in love with you when he came home following your first meeting. After he told me how beautiful you were and how talented, he went off to his room whistling. It was the first time I'd ever heard him whistle."

II To Honor and to Cherish

WHAT IS MARRIAGE?

Marriage is the union
       of two people in love,
And love is sheer magic
       for it's woven of
Gossamer dreams,
       enchantingly real,
That people in love
       are privileged to feel—
But the "exquisite ecstasy"
       that captures the heart
Of two people in love
       is just a small part
Of the beauty and wonder
       and *miracle* of
The growth and fulfillment
       and evolvement of love—
For only long years
       of living together
And sharing and caring
       in all kinds of weather
Both pleasure and pain,
       the glad and the sad,
Teardrops and laughter,
       the good and the bad,
Can add new dimensions
       and lift love above
The rapturous ecstasies
       of "falling in love"—
For ecstasy passes
       but it is replaced
By something much greater
       that cannot be defaced,

> For what was "in part"
> has now "become whole"—
> For on the "wings of the flesh,"
> love entered the "soul"!

*O*n January 30, 1929, Franklin and I were married in New York City's historic Marble Collegiate Church. The ceremony was performed by the Reverend Daniel Poling. Gertrude was my maid of honor and Elwood was Franklin's best man. Afterward, we went to Elwood's suite at the Plaza Hotel. It was as exquisitely and expensively furnished as his mansion on Long Island.

Elwood's home reminded me of a medieval castle with its fine furnishings, paintings, silver, and servants. There were people to take care of every need. Once, when we visited Elwood and his wife, I remember needing a dress pressed. When I asked one of the maids where I could find an iron, I was directed to the basement, where I proceeded to do my own ironing.

"Please tell Helen not to do that again," Elwood told my husband when he learned of my social faux pas. "The servants won't understand."

To say that I was uncomfortable in such affluence is putting it mildly. I found it suffocating. Fortunately, in Dayton I was allowed to run my own house with very little outside help. That is not to say I couldn't have had several servants had I wanted them.

Franklin may not have been worth as much as his New York brother, but he had more wealth than I'd ever imagined. Our honeymoon cruise had been in the Caribbean, and we returned to Ohio for the next two years where we had a huge fourteen-room house on a large estate with three expensive cars in the drive—a big LaSalle, a Cadillac, and a Packard. We lived a wonderful, carefree life. We vacationed at the finest places, traveled, when Franklin's work at the bank permitted, partied, and in general "lived it up." Oh, there was some little flap about an economic downturn, but Franklin (who was a whiz with figures) assured me that Hoover would soon get the country back on its feet.

In fact, Franklin was so sure that the country's business problems were short-term that he invested more heavily in the stock market.

"Great time to buy," he told me. "Bernard Baruch always says to buy your straw hats in September not May, and now's the time to buy when prices are so low." I knew nothing about the market, only that the Depression deepened and many well-to-do people lost everything. Though Franklin may have been worried, he never gave me any inkling of how desperate he was. I had heard about paper millionaires throwing themselves out of windows because of lost fortunes, and had thought, *How utterly preposterous!*

Then, one day I came home from playing bridge with some of the ladies at the club and learned the horrible news. Franklin had gone to the garage, closed the doors, started one of the cars, and died of carbon-monoxide poisoning.

The note he left behind spelled out his woes:

> Darling, the only thing I'm sorry about is that I never could give you all the things I meant to. I hope you believe that I really wanted to give them to you, and I could have given them to you before everything went . . . Keep the picture of me in my uniform and think of me once in a while . . . You'll get along fine, I know. You'll always go on. I only knew one world. I just can't go down and become a bum—I have to go out with the band playing.

For the second time, the man in my life had been taken from me. First, it was my wonderful father when I was eighteen and now, at age thirty-one, my loving husband.

Again I cried out to God, *Why?* and again I heard nothing but the lonely echo of my own voice.

Part II:
The Middle Years

12 *A New Start*

THERE IS A REASON FOR EVERYTHING

Our Father knows what's best for us,
So why should we complain—
We always want the sunshine,
But He knows there must be rain—
We love the sound of laughter
And the merriment of cheer,
But our hearts would lose their tenderness
If we never shed a tear . . .
Our Father tests us often
With suffering and with sorrow,
He tests us, not to punish us,
But to help us meet TOMORROW . . .
For growing trees are strengthened
When they withstand the storm,
And the sharp cut of the chisel
Gives the marble grace and form . . .
God never hurts us needlessly,
And He never wastes our pain,
For every loss He sends to us
Is followed by rich gain . . .
And when we count the blessings
That God has so freely sent,
We will find no cause for murmuring
And no time to lament
For Our Father loves His children,
And to Him all things are plain,
So He never sends us PLEASURES
When the SOUL'S DEEP NEED IS PAIN . . .
So whenever we are troubled,
And when everything goes wrong,
It is just God working in us
To make OUR SPIRIT STRONG.

What was left of our estate was auctioned off to pay creditors, and I soon found myself ready to go back to work.

Unlike some widows, I had made my way in the world of business before, so I had no fear of starving. But where should I begin? Something in me said that I was on the threshold of a new adventure. All I know is that after recovering from the shock of Franklin's death, I was filled with the positive feeling that God was going to bring something good out of all this. "All things work together for good to them that love God, to them who are the called according to his purpose" (Romans 8:28) I told myself again and again.

In the spring of 1931, I moved to Cincinnati. I say "moved." That is a misnomer. After paying off our bills, I was left with little more than my wardrobe (some very fine clothes, I might add), a few mementos, and the vague feeling that my dreamlike marriage to Franklin had been just that—a dream.

I had once told Franklin the story of a young girl who stood at the edge of a huge field of corn. Far as she could see, beautiful green stalks heavy with corn waved in the gentle breeze.

A genie told the girl, "If you walk into the field, I will reward you with a gift in proportion to the size of the ear you choose. Start where you are and begin walking. You can go through the field only once and you may not go back and retrace your steps. And you cannot trade one ear for another once you have picked one. Bring your selection with you to the other side of the field and there you'll receive your reward."

As she walked, the girl shunned ears on stalks of the outside rows, imagining the corn in the middle of the field to be the biggest. So she waited, hoping to find a huge ear and gain an equally huge reward.

Carefree she walked, oblivious to time or location. When she came to her senses, however, she saw the ears had suddenly grown smaller. Raising her head and looking behind, she realized she had come a long way. Ahead, she saw the end of the field. In desperation, she touched one ear, then another, but they were all smaller by far than thousands she had passed by.

"Oh, there must be one more big ear before the end," she cried. But there wasn't, and she emerged from the field empty-handed.

Though I had come "out of the cornfield" with nothing much in the way of material goods to launch a new life, I had my mind, my enthusiasm, my health, my creativity, and my faith. With those assets, I set sail again.

Whenever I'd visited Cincinnati before, during my speaking days, I'd always stayed at the Netherland Plaza, so out of habit I moved in there. But in a matter of days, I met an old friend, Sam Heed, who had been an executive in the utility industry. He'd come to Cincinnati and become a vice-president for the Gibson Art Company, a publisher of greeting cards.

"I want you to stay at the Gibson Hotel," he said. "I have a fine apartment for you."

I protested that I wasn't exactly rolling in cash, but he refused to listen. "Come over and see for yourself. If you like the apartment, I'll send a truck for your things in the morning."

The accommodations were ideal, and I agreed to accept Sam Heed's offer—temporarily. I had no idea *temporary* meant the next forty-two years!

Here I am at age three.

My wonderful mother, Anna Bieri
Steiner.

As I graduated from Lorain High School.

When I first went to work for the Electric Light and Power Company of Lorain, I prayed to be a dynamo!

About 1925, when I was traveling coast to coast as a public speaker.

My sister Gertrude, about the same time.

Franklin Rice was a major in the air corps during World War I. He flew many combat missions.

Franklin and I, the night before our wedding at New York's Marble Collegiate Church in 1929.

Our wedding certificate signed by Dr. Daniel A. Poling.

Shortly after I became editor of the Gibson Art Company in Cincinnati.

I love to travel. This picture was taken aboard the *Normandie* in July 1939. The war clouds were gathering.

After World War II, I was able to resume ocean liner vacations. This was taken in 1946.

With the famous "Praying Hands" exhibit.

Here is my "pen pal" and longtime friend, Kathleen Mimms of Newport, Kentucky.

13 A Gibson Girl

AFTER THE WINTER GOD SENDS SPRING

Springtime is a season
            Of Hope and Joy and Cheer,
There's beauty all around us
            To see and touch and hear . . .
So, no matter how downhearted
            And discouraged we may be,
New Hope is born when we behold
            Leaves budding on a tree . . .
Or when we see a timid flower
            Push through the frozen sod
And open wide in glad surprise
            Its petaled eyes to God . . .
For this is just God saying—
            "Lift up your eyes to Me,
And the bleakness of your spirit,
            Like the budding springtime tree,
Will lose its wintry darkness
            And your heavy heart will sing"—
For God never sends the Winter
            Without the Joy of Spring

*I*n order to earn a living, I had returned to the speaking circuit, and I soon had as many opportunities to give talks as I could handle. But one day Mr. Heed asked me to have lunch with him and consider a different profession.

"I'd like you to come to work at Gibson's," he said.

"In what capacity?" I asked.

"As a troubleshooter," he answered. "We're hurting from the Depression like everyone else. Review our company from top to bottom. With your wide experience, you're bound to come up with some helpful suggestions."

When I protested that I knew nothing about the greeting card business, he would hear none of it.

"When do you want to begin?" A week later I came to work. The story

59

of Gibson Greeting Cards Inc.—as the company is known today—is another fascinating episode of realized business opportunity in America. When George Gibson decided to move his wife and family of nine children from England to the United States in 1850, it was a huge undertaking. They had few possessions and little money, but they had lofty dreams. George's business hopes were transported in a large wooden crate which contained a French-made lithograph press. The press, which had been the keystone of a small printing business in England, was shipped to New York, and then to Cincinnati by canals.

Five of George Gibson's sons were printers and four of them settled in Cincinnati. The oldest son chose Detroit and father, mother, and daughters took residence in Saint Louis. The boys who founded the Gibson Company were Stephen, Robert, George, and Samuel.

For the first few years, the company was engaged in commercial printing—stock and bond certificates, checks, business cards, advertising brochures, and so on. When the Civil War broke out, Gibson and Company produced stationery for writing letters to the boys off doing the fighting. It was not until 1880, thirty years after its founding, that the company first began distributing fringed Christmas cards imported from Germany. The cards were popular, so the Gibson brothers decided to design, print, and sell their own. They never regretted the decision. In nearly one hundred years since, they have become one of the largest producers of greeting cards in the world.

However, the Depression had drastically reduced the company's business. Still, when I came to work, I was surprised to learn that millions of people sent all-occasion cards even in hard times. Though many were broke, out of work or on government programs like WPA or CCC, they kept their sense of humor and passed their hopefulness along via greeting cards.

As the words of a popular song of those days expressed it, Americans could laugh together and say:

> Oh! we ain't got a barrel of money,
> Maybe we're ragged and funny,
> But we'll travel along
> Singin' a song Side By Side.

I found the work at Gibson the ideal tonic for the loneliness of widowhood, and I threw myself into the job with all my resources. I bombarded management with long memos, asking questions and making suggestions. With no experience in the business and being new, I asked many naïve questions, I am sure, but some of them caused people to rethink procedures that had been taken for granted for years. Nothing was sacrosanct: production, selling, design, editorial, billing, customer relations, anything and everything that came to my attention I investigated.

Sam Heed was delighted with my reports. Once when I returned from a business trip, I brought him a list of sales-incentive ideas as long as my arm.

"Helen, where do you get all your energy?" he asked.

"From my mountain-climbing Swiss ancestors!" I answered.

About a year after I joined Gibson's, its editor, Ethel Brainerd, died suddenly and the company needed someone to select, write, and edit verses for its greeting cards. I was asked if I'd like the job. Again, I had to confess a lack of experience in this particular line, though it was true that I'd written verses for publication since I was in high school.

However, all assured me I could do the job, so I agreed to try. Once again as I look back on my life, I see God's Hand quietly leading, quietly clearing the way for events over which I had little or no control.

14 *Writer of Verses*

THE ANATOMY OF A GREETING CARD

You've read what the different departments do,
Now here's a "summarized rhyme" for you . . .
In short, it's just a bird's-eye view
Of what a Greeting Card goes through . . .
You've no idea how much work it requires
To make a card that the public desires,
We're sure that none of you surmised
And that you'll all be very surprised
To follow the Birth of a Gibson Greeting
At Our Hundredth Anniversary Meeting:
In the Birth of a Card the First Operation
Is, as it should be, "An Act of Creation" . . .
So, on the 4th floor, in the Department of Art,
Some artist gives a Card its start,
A little paint and a clever line
And the artist presents a new design . . .
From there it leaves the scene of art
And goes to get itself a "heart"—
For any card without a greeting
Is like a visit without a meeting,
So down to the Editorial it goes
For a sentiment written in rhyme or prose,
Then the Numbering and Estimate fellows step in
And order the quantity required to begin,
Work Sheets are written and Records compiled
And Drawings are made and Lettering is styled,
The Layout Department then figures the "sheet"
And makes a "layout" that's neat and complete,
Then the Engravers and Plate Makers start
And contribute their most essential part,
Then the Card goes to the Printing Floor
And the powerful presses begin to roar . . .
From here cards go to the Die-Maker's place
And "die-outs" are made to take care of each case,
Then back to the Press Room to be Cut-Out and Sized
In a manner that leaves you amazed and surprised,
Then the Caption is Stamped and the Card is ready

To take on the glamour of Hollywood's Hedy . . .
Silk Screening, Flocking, Embossing and Flitter
Are added to give the Card glamour and glitter,
Then cards are Folded by hand or machine
And carefully done so they stay white and clean,
Then a Sample's Assembled and from this one
The entire "run" is fashioned and done,
Ribbon, Sachet and Satin and Lace
Are put on by hand, by girls in the place,
Then cards are Checked, O.K.'d and Inspected
So any errors can be detected . . .
Now they are ready for the last, final touch,
That consists of Boxing and Labeling and such,
Then on to the Shipping Room bunks to be stacked
Until it is time for them to be packed,
And where the Card is shipped and lands
Is in some Super-Salesman's hands
Its Destiny rests in the Dealer's Display,
Where the Passing Parade goes by it each day,
And who can tell and who can guess
How great is its power for happiness . . .
And so your loved ones have had a part
In reaching and touching the "Nation's Heart"—
And Friendship and Love and Goodwill on Earth
Are kept alive through the Greeting Card's Birth.
                    (written to mark Gibson's 100th Anniversary.)

*I*n the midthirties when I became editor at Gibson's, greeting card messages tended, for the most part, to be light and cheery, often humorous. Especially frowned upon were sentiments of an inspirational or religious flavor. They were thought to have no place in the lineup of cards offered by a major greeting card company, and, for the time being, I did nothing to change that policy.

My first few years were spent developing shorter, smoother, warmer, snappier verses, and the company said the results were very good. I also made design and art suggestions in an attempt to harmonize the visual part of a greeting card with its editorial message. For Gibson's 100th Anniversary celebration I wrote the poem at the beginning of this chapter about the "birth" of a greeting card, explaining the steps needed to make it successful. The customer, of course, is the one who determines the outcome with his or her purchase. If popular, the card may stay in production for many years. Often verses and art are changed around to give something old a new look. Like fashions, the look of art changes from year to year.

Speaking of fashion, I suppose my mother's love of clothes, her style sense, her love of colors, was inherited by me. Whatever, it gave me an advantage when I entered the greeting card business.

Of course, like most jobs, mine included some administration. Record keeping, correspondence, sales meetings, dealing with authors and in-house personnel occupied a good deal of my time.

One of the ongoing challenges of editors in a greeting card company is finding new writers who are able to bring a fresh dimension to their work—people who can spin a phrase and compose with a flair for words. Finding new talent is always rewarding, and over the years I've discovered a good many skilled writers of greeting-card verse.

A few. times, though, I've been fooled by impostors, writers who "borrow" from others and present poems as their own original work. Accidents do happen, though, and writers do crib lines from previously written works subconsciously. However, it sometimes is nothing short of plagiarism.

I once received some exceptionally good lines from a person who wrote under a pseudonym. He became something of a notorious case around the company, because eventually we noticed a similarity between the verses we had bought from him and others appearing on the cards of other companies.

He had represented himself to Gibson as an engineer with a distinguished New England family background. But about the time our Sherlock Holmeses caught on to his ruse, he vanished. Investigation at the bank used to cash our checks led us to believe "he" might even have been a she. Whatever, we were left with some plagiarized poems and no trace of what we thought was a budding verse writer.

Looking back over my records, I located some of my compositions at the time to give you an idea of the verses I was writing. As was the case with almost all greeting-card contributors, none of my rhymes was signed.

A Valentine to Someone
I Haven't Forgotten
I may not see you often
    Or write you as I should—
But forget you is one of the things
I never would or could.

———

Best Wishes to a "Model" Dad
on Father's Day
Father's Day is one of those days
That Dads like you deserve some praise,
And this is coming just to say

*You're wished a happy Father's Day,
And you're so dear and thoughtful, too,
More Dads should be "modeled" after you.*

---

*A Christmas Reflection
It's kinda nice to reminisce
When Christmas lights are glowing
And think about the folks like you
Who are so worthwhile knowing.*

---

*Thinking of You
on Sweetest Day
Thinking of someone
as nice as you
Is always pleasant
and so nice to do,
And on a day
like Sweetest Day
It's just a happy time
to say
The world would be better
and nicer by far
If all the folks in it
were as nice as you are.*

As you can see, there was nothing in these sentiments that could be considered inspirational. But I was writing inspirational verses privately, even then, ones which were sent to friends on birthdays, anniversaries, and special occasions. They were God-given thoughts that flowed from the heart, that blessed me the writer and seemed to be appreciated by the recipients. But none of those faith-affirming poems worked its way into the Gibson line for more than twenty-five years.

"Why?" some ask me.

"Simply because the time wasn't right," I answer. It was too soon for God's timetable. Always remember, God is never too early nor too late, but He always acts when the time is right. Things occur, I believe, as I wrote in a poem "Not by Chance nor Happenstance."

> Into our lives come many things
> to break the dull routine,

The things we had not planned on
   that happen unforeseen,
The unexpected little joys
   that are scattered on our way,
Success we did not count on
   or a rare, fulfilling day—
A catchy, lilting melody
   that makes us want to dance,
A nameless exaltation
   of enchantment and romance—
An unsought word of kindness,
   a compliment or two
That sets the eyes to gleaming
   like crystal drops of dew—
The unplanned sudden meeting
   that comes with sweet surprise
And lights the heart with happiness
   like a rainbow in the skies . . .
Now some folks call it fickle fate
   and some folks call it chance,
While others just accept it
   as pleasant happenstance—
But no matter what you call it
   it didn't come without design,
For all our lives are fashioned
   by the HAND THAT IS DIVINE—
And every happy happening
   and every lucky break
Are little gifts from God above
   that are ours to freely take.

15 *We Never Walk Alone*

WHAT MORE CAN WE ASK?

What more can we ask of the Saviour
Than to know we are never alone—
That His Mercy and Love are
    unfailing
And He makes all our problems His
    Own.

*T*hose early years at Gibson's—in particular the thirties and forties— were very happy ones for me, very busy ones, very fulfilling ones. Although some people looked upon me as something of a "mysterious" person, I know, probably because I threw myself so wholeheartedly into my work at the expense of all else, it was my choice and my way to enjoyment.

"Are you ever going to remarry?" friends would ask me. I responded, "Not unless someone very, very special comes along." The fact that I didn't wed again is self-explanatory. Not that I didn't have opportunities. Being a woman in her thirties, possessing passable looks, being a stylish dresser and the executive of a large corporation gave me an opportunity to meet and date a good many eligible and handsome bachelors, but as I said, I was choosy, and most of my time was work-directed.

Some people misunderstood my life and tried to paint a picture of a tragically lonely lady. Once a Cincinnati magazine column did an anonymous sketch about me that probably added fuel to the "mystery lady" image.

The sidewalk cafe is filled with people . . . parties of men and women chatting through dinner . . . couples smiling at each other . . . here and there a lone man with a newspaper for a dinner companion . . . while over all drifts pleasantly soothing organ music.

Suddenly the music changes. It gains a lilting rhythm which before it seemed to lack. To a special table near the organist comes,

escorted by the headwaiter, the Lady with the Hat. Heads turn and
all eyes survey the creation of the evening.

It may be a misty thing of flowers, violets perhaps, or while lilacs
with a froth of dainty veiling and cleverly placed ribbon, or perhaps
it's a handsome sweep of feathers . . . Sometimes her hat is made of
felt or velvet or taffeta, but with a certain perfection of style and
color which seems to make all other hats quite dismal by compari-
son. Always it is new, eye-catching and as charming as the lady
who wears it.

But "The Lady with the Hat" didn't spend all her time dining alone. I
was involved in many activities. I often played bridge with friends for
one thing. I was also active in Republician politics (being particularly
involved in some of Mayor W. D. Gradison, Sr., and Senator Robert A.
Taft's campaigns). The fact that Taft was passed over for the presidential
nomination was one of my big disappointments. He was a man of great
integrity and wisdom, and I believe would have been a truly outstanding president.

I also attended Wesley Methodist Chapel regularly, though I kept my
church membership in Lorain. When members of the Lorain church
were locked in debate over whether to build a new church or not (the
older members for the most part were "agin" it and the younger ones for
it), I mounted my soapbox and sided with those who wanted to build.
The vote was in favor of the new edifice and today the beautiful Meister
Road Church is thriving.

All of this time I was living in an apartment on the seventh floor of the
Gibson, an apartment that Ida Lee ("Mom") Ginn kept in order. I must
tell you about Mom, one of the loves of my life.

When I moved into the Gibson, they sent me a maid to clean my
apartment each day while I was at work. But the first one was less than
satisfactory and in her place they sent Ida Lee Ginn, a slight woman in
her forties with a bright look in her eyes, a broad smile on her face, and a
Kentucky short'nin'-bread drawl that could have charmed Scrooge out of
his watch fob.

Though I didn't know it at the time, Ida Lee had more on the ball than
the rest of the hotel's housekeeping staff put together. Whenever a celebrity was a guest, she managed to get the assignment of cleaning the
suite. Whether it was the president, royalty, or foreign dignitaries, she
prevailed and got the job. And what a job she did. She didn't just make
the beds and sweep. She rearranged flowers, sent clothes out for press-
ing, ordered meals, sewed on buttons—anything that made the guest's
stay a better one. As a result, she earned more tips than any of the other
maids—and made more friends, too.

What a lucky day it was for me when "Mom," as I was soon calling her, came into my life. She had a family of her own to care for, which she did with loving concern, despite the fact that she put in eight hours a day at the hotel, seven days a week. But she never complained. All her life, Mom has taken one day at a time.

Anyway, she became a very special person in my life, and I took a great interest in her family. When holidays came, we often shared them. Whatever needs Mom had, I gave them my attention, and Mom tried to help me with my burdens, too.

Few people have had a closer relationship with their maid than I had with Mom who worked for me for forty-four years, until she retired in 1976. I'll never forget the reaction of one hotel guest when I said good-bye to her one day. It was my custom to go down the hall of my floor, before going off to work, to kiss Mom good-bye. One day a businessman observed me—dressed to the nines—giving her a hug and kiss and telling her, "I'll see you after work, Mom."

"Why does that rich woman allow her mother to work as a maid?" he asked at the front desk!

I suppose my affection for Mom Ginn could be summed up in this birthday greeting I sent her in 1972. I'm big on birthday poems for my friends, and in addition to a birthday gift, Mom has gotten a personal rhyme from me for more than forty years:

> There is no way to tell you
>   how much you mean to me . . .
> I only know I'm THANKFUL
>   that God sent me Ida Lee,
> And I only know I'm GRATEFUL
>   that Our Father Up Above
> Made You "My Guardian Angel"
>   and gave me you to Love . . .
> And just between the two of us,
>   each time I look at you,
> I can't Believe "My Pretty Mom"
>   is really EIGHTY-TWO,
> For years may come and years may go
>   but you WILL ALWAYS BE
> The Same Dear Little Lady
>   Mr. Braden brought to me . . .
> Now may the Good Lord BLESS YOU
>   and Keep you in HIS CARE
> And I will ask Him every day
>   when I go to Him in prayer

That when He gently calls to you
   and says, "Come unto Me,"
He'll also say to Helen Rice,
   "You come along with Ida Lee" . . .
And that will be a "Glad Reunion"
   when I introduce you to
My darling "Little Mother"
   who reminds me, Dear, of you!

16 *A Time for Sorrow*

TEACH US TO LIVE

God of love—Forgive! Forgive!
Teach us how to TRULY LIVE,
Ask us not our race or creed,
Just take us in our hour of need,
And let us know You love us, too,
And that we are A PART OF YOU . . .
And someday may man realize
That all the earth, the seas and skies
Belong to God who made us all,
The rich, the poor, the great, the small,
And in the Father's Holy Sight
No man is yellow, black or white,
And PEACE ON EARTH cannot be found
Until we MEET ON COMMON GROUND
And every man becomes a BROTHER
Who worships God and loves each other.

One of my avocations is travel, and in my lifetime I have visited countries in all parts of the world. In addition to its providing me with relaxation, I have learned a great deal about the history, geography, religions, and cultural practices of different peoples through my many excursions.

But one trip, a cruise on the liner *Vulcania* which took me and my traveling companions, Mrs. Sam Heed and Mrs. Mark Curran, to the Mediterranean in 1936, taught me something else: a world war was imminent.

Battleships bearing the flags of England, France, and Italy seemed to be everywhere. Troop movements and shipping activity were being observed closely, and port security was unusually tight. All was a portent of things to come.

We all have our memories of World War II—the separations, sacrifices, and sorrow. At the Gibson Greeting Card Company, many of our employees went off to fight or to work in defense plants. Meanwhile, the rest of us turned our attention to publishing greetings that reflected the

71

mood of the times. Demand for cards to cheer servicemen and women far from home nearly doubled during the war years. In 1942, Gibson printed more than 30 million Christmas cards, a huge increase from the prewar years. Many of them carried a patriotic motif, decorated with American flags, crests, and other red, white, and blue symbols. Many birthday and anniversary cards also featured patriotic and "God and country" themes. One card I remember had Uncle Sam on the cover, while another carried a drawing of the Statue of Liberty. Anything with a flag on it was popular, including one stars-and-bars pin that could be removed from the card and worn on one's lapel.

I wrote many thousands of verses for cards during the war years, and for the first time rhymes of a more serious nature were in huge demand. Of course, cards with clever humor were still sent, but positive, inspiring, faith-affirming greetings were well received by an audience sobered by the realities of war.

The war touched everyone in one way or another. One of Mom Ginn's sons, Jackie, served in the Pacific Theater. Every Sunday morning, before I went off to church, Mom and I got down on our knees and prayed that the Lord would watch over her son.

"Oh, I couldn't bear it if something happened to him," she said.

"God will keep him in the palm of His Hand," I assured her. "He shall give His angels charge over him," I told her, paraphrasing Saint Luke (4:10, 11). "And in their hands they shall bear him up, lest at any time he would dash his foot against a stone."

But when word came that Jackie had been wounded in battle, Mom came to me in tears.

"I'm not going to pray any more if that's the kind of God He is," Mom cried.

"Oh, but you are," I answered, pulling her down to her knees with me. "Not only are you and I going to pray, but we're going to pray harder than ever!" A few months later Jackie came home, safe and sound.

When the war was over, I wrote a poem for our company paper, *Gibsonews,* which I edited, and which we sent to employees serving their country. Its message is still appropriate:

> Peace dawns once more on a war-torn earth
> While a world gone wild with hysteria and mirth
> Raises its voice in loud jubilation
> To try to express its heart's exultation . . .
> Cities and towns and country places
> Became just a seething sea of faces,
> Prayers, thanksgiving and unchecked tears
> Mingled with thunderous and unrestrained cheers . . .

Four days we had lived between war and peace
Waiting and watching for war to cease
And now in this hour of triumphal thanksgiving
We pray for the Dead and give thanks for the Living . . .
May we never forget those who sleep 'neath the sod,
They helped liberate, by the grace of our God;
We've reached at long last the Victor's Goal
But to keep THE PEACE we must conquer our soul,
We have wrestled and vanquished the Enemy
But we enter a "new Gethsemane" . . .
The struggle now enters a realm deep within
And each man has his own private battle to win
And the words of Christ ring out in our ears
Amid the tumult of Victory Cheers;
And the Unknown Soldier pleads to be heard
And his message is told in Christ's stirring word
"Ye Must Be Born Again" or we the slain
Have fought and fallen and died in vain . . .
Keep us grateful, Omnipotent God,
And aware of those sleeping beneath the sod,
Strengthen our bonds one with another
So we may dwell as brother to brother,
Heal the wounds and be with us yet,
Lest we forget! Lest we forget!

Not long before the end of World War II, Mother died in Lorain. She passed away February 20, 1945, at age seventy-three.

When the minister asked if Gertrude or I had any special instructions for her funeral service, I handed him a poem I'd written immediately after learning of her death. It was titled "When I Must Leave You."

When I must leave you
  for a little while,
Please do not grieve
  and shed wild tears
And hug your sorrow
  to you through the years,
But start out bravely
  with a gallant smile;
And for my sake
  and in my name
Live on and do
  all the things the same,

Feed not your loneliness
  on empty days,
But fill each waking hour
  in useful ways,
Reach out your hand
  in comfort and in cheer
And I in turn will comfort you
  and hold you near;
And never, never
  be afraid to die,
For I am waiting
  for you in the sky!

When he finished reading it, he turned to me with tears in his eyes and said, "With your permission, I'd like to build my message around it." And he did. Though the poem has been one of the readers' favorites over the years, and I have received thousands of letters praising me for the sentiment, I cannot take credit for it. The thought expressed is my mother's. She told me many times not to grieve when she died, but to go on in faith until our reunion in heaven. I'm looking forward to that day.

17 *Verses for My Friends*

THANK GOD FOR LITTLE THINGS

Thank You, God, for little things
      that often come our way—
The things we take for granted
      but don't mention when we pray—
The unexpected courtesy,
      the thoughtful, kindly deed—
A hand reached out to help us
      in the time of sudden need—
Oh, make us more aware, dear God,
      of little daily graces
That come to us with "sweet surprise"
      from never-dreamed-of places.

Once a woman in Massachusetts made the claim that she was the champion verse writer with over one hundred thousand verses composed in twenty-four years. Some of my co-workers took umbrage, knowing that my output far exceeds that. In fact, some people who like to engage in such statistics once figured that in my heyday I was averaging over 250 verses a day, which came out to 75,000 plus a year. Considering I got into the business in 1931 and worked steadily at it for nearly 40 years, my total probably reached more than 2 million verses. Only a few hundred were signed; most of my rhymes appeared anonymously.

Not all of the poems I wrote were published, of course, but thousands worked their way into the Gibson line each year; others were retired to that home of rejected verse: that "circular file on the floor," the wastebasket.

In addition, there were many personal poems that I wrote for my friends, little special-occasion greetings. A check of my files reveals examples such as these:

CONGRATULATIONS

Your marriage has been truly blessed
For with your new son's birth,
God sent an Angel down from Heaven

To live with you on earth
For I think God UP IN HEAVEN
Looks down on couples in love
And blesses their happy union
With a Gift of His Love FROM ABOVE . . .
And so through this Tiny Angel
He has drawn you together for life,
For now you are Father and Mother
Instead of just husband and wife . . .
And while he is yours to fondle,
To care for, to teach, and to love,
He belongs to His Father IN HEAVEN,
For he came from His Home UP ABOVE . . .
So ask Him for guidance in molding
The future of your little boy,
For he is a "Jewel" from His Kingdom
Sent to bring you Heavenly Joy!

FOR A WONDERFUL SIS

If I knew the place
          WHERE WISHES COME TRUE,
That's where I would go
          for My Wish For You . . .
And I'd wish you all
          that YOU'RE WISHING FOR,
For no sister on earth
          deserves it more . . .
But trials and troubles
          come to us all,
For that's the way
          we grow "Heaven Tall" . . .
And My Birthday Prayer
          to Our Father Above
Is to Keep You Safe
          In His Infinite Love,
And we both know that
          GIFTS DON'T MEAN MUCH
Compared to "Our Love"
          and God's Blessed Touch!

FOR A CO-WORKER

For your wisdom and your friendship,
       your counsel and advice . . .
You've won the admiration
       of Helen Steiner Rice . . .
And as the years go hurrying by
       I pause and think anew
How fortunate I was to meet
       a kind, wise friend like you . . .
And I'm but one of many
       who owe a lot to you . . .
For all the help you've given
       and time and effort too . . .
And this is just a welcome chance
       to tell you that you've won . . .
The only REAL SUCCESS in life
       by the FINE THINGS you have done.

AN ANNIVERSARY WISH

As you recall that happy day
       that united you in love,
May you read this book together
       as The Lord smiles from above
And blesses you especially
       because through Faith and Prayer
You Took Him for a Partner
       and placed Your Marriage in His Care,
For is was by Divine Design
       that you two met each other
And then God made you "Man and Wife"
       and a loving Dad and Mother!

FOR MY DOCTOR

Don't think, because I don't come back,
That I'm Dissatisfied . . .
It's just because the truth I sought
Was fully gratified . . .
You can't Hold Back the Dawn
Or Stop the Tides from Flowing
Or Keep a Rose from Withering
Or Still a Wind that's Blowing . . .

And there's No Pill
      at any Price
To *Turn Back Time*
      and make a *"Younger Rice"*!

Some of the poems that I wrote strictly for friends later made their way into print. I'll never forget the night I paused on my way out the door of Gibson's. The sun was setting and its golden light was reflecting off the office windows behind. A co-worker, Ed Gunther, standing beside me said, "I'll never forget the story you told the Gibson salesman about the windows of gold." It prompted me to put the legend into rhyme:

THE WINDOWS OF GOLD

There is a legend that has often been told
Of the boy who searched for THE WIN-
      DOWS OF GOLD,
The beautiful windows he saw far away
When he looked in the valley at sunrise
      each day,
And he yearned to go down to the valley
      below
But he lived on a mountain that was cov-
      ered with snow
And he knew it would be a difficult trek,
But that was a journey he wanted to
      make,
So he planned by day and he dreamed
      by night
Of how he could reach THE GREAT
      SHINING LIGHT . . .
And one golden morning when dawn
      broke through
And the valley sparkled with diamonds
      of dew
He started to climb down the mountain-
      side
With THE WINDOWS OF GOLD as his
      goal and his guide . . .
He traveled all day and, weary and worn,
With bleeding feet and clothes that were
      torn

He entered the peaceful valley town
Just as the golden sun went down . . .
But he seemed to have lost his "GUID-
        ING LIGHT,"
The windows were dark that had once
        been bright,
And hungry and tired and lonely and
        cold
He cried, "WON'T YOU SHOW ME THE
        WINDOWS OF GOLD?"
And a kind hand touched him and
        said, "BEHOLD, HIGH ON THE
        MOUNTAIN ARE THE WINDOWS
        OF GOLD"—
For the sun going down in a great golden
        ball
Had burnished the windows of his cabin
        so small,
And THE KINGDOM OF GOD with its
        GREAT SHINING LIGHT,
Like the Golden Windows that shone so
        bright,
Is not a far distant place somewhere,
It's as close to you as a silent prayer—
And your search for God will end and
        begin
When you look for HIM and FIND HIM
        WITHIN.

One day during the late 1950s, my friend Bill Dressman, vice-president at Gibson, came to me with some sales figures on the cards which carried my verses.

"They really like your poems, Helen," he said, "and I think you should sign some of these outstanding sellers."

I told Bill that I was pleased to hear that I was appreciated, but that I didn't really need any public recognition of my work to make me happy.

"I'm just another worker in the vineyard, trying to do His will," I told him. "My calling seems to be putting old spiritual truths into simple little rhymes."

"Well, simple or not, people like them, and I think they should know who composes them. Furthermore, I'm going to talk to management about the matter. I think people would be even more responsive to your verses, if they knew the person behind them."

The next season, a few cards were signed Helen Steiner Rice, something that is seldom done in the greeting-card business. To my surprise, people were interested in the author.

Then Bill Dressman had another idea: to put a dozen or so of my poems together in a small booklet. He wanted to print ten thousand copies, but our sales manager thought the number too high. So he queried the Gibson sales force. They were enthusiastic, so the print order stood—for a few weeks. Then we had to go back to press, for the orders were up to twenty-two thousand copies and growing.

I didn't have any idea of the excitement that lay just ahead. But God knew, of course, and as always I just followed along, willing to let Him show me the next step in His plan for my life.

The Welk Connection

THE PRICELESS GIFT OF CHRISTMAS

Now Christmas is a season
        for joy and merrymaking,
A time for gifts and presents,
        for giving and for taking . . .
A festive, friendly happy time
        when everyone is gay—
But have we ever really felt
        the *greatness of the day* . . .
For through the centuries the world
        has wandered far away
From the beauty and the meaning
        of the *Holy Christmas Day* . . .
For Christmas is a heavenly gift
        that only God can give,
It's ours just for the asking,
        for as long as we shall live . . .
It can't be bought or bartered,
        it can't be won or sold,
It doesn't cost a penny
        and it's worth far more than gold . . .
It isn't bright and gleaming
        for eager eyes to see,
It can't be wrapped in tinsel
        or placed beneath a tree . . .
It isn't soft and shimmering
        for reaching hands to touch,
Or some expensive luxury
        you've wanted very much . . .
For the *priceless Gift of Christmas*
        is meant just for the heart
And we receive it only
        when we become a part
Of the kingdom and the glory
        which is ours to freely take,
For God sent the Holy Christ Child
        at Christmas for our sake,

So man might come to know *Him*
          and feel *His Presence* near
And see the many miracles
          performed while *He* was here . . .
And this *priceless Gift of Christmas*
          is within the reach of all,
The rich, the poor, the young and old
          the greatest and the small . . .
So take *His Priceless Gift of Love,*
          reach out and you receive,
And the only payment that God asks
          is just that *you believe.*

*O*n the Lawrence Welk television show shortly before Christmas in 1960, one of his entertainers, a talented person who performed under the stage name *Aladdin,* gave a reading of a Christmas greeting he had received from his sister.

Aladdin didn't know that I was the author, so the verse was not credited, but the response from listeners who wanted to obtain copies of it was so strong that the show's producers came looking for the source of "The Priceless Gift of Christmas."

In one fell swoop, millions of people had been touched by a simple poem that told the old, old story of God's sending His only Son to save mankind. It was the culmination of one of my dreams, really. For as long as I could remember, I had wanted to spread the Gospel of His love, not by preachments but by quiet verses of inspiration. I had no idea how God would allow me to be an instrument of His, but since childhood I'd had the feeling in my heart that if I was faithful to Him, He would use me in a magnificent way.

For a long time, as I've told you, people in the industry were not interested in inspirational poems. They thought they were too sentimental and specialized to sell, but with the publicity that came from Aladdin's reading, demand for my inspirational verses took off like a rocket.

"Don't you have some other inspirational things in your files?" the Gibson people wanted to know.

"Yes, I've got a few verses on prayer and faith and God's love," I told them. For the most part they were greetings I had sent to personal friends, but one by one I brought them out of their dusty folders.

In 1961, Aladdin read another of my poems on television. It was called "Praying Hands," and was about Albrecht Dürer's famous painting.

I'd once read an inspiring story about Dürer's friend, who was himself an aspiring artist. Because they were both starving, Dürer's friend volunteered to go to work, until they both could afford to pursue their ambitions. However, the work the friend chose to do was hard and it took its toll—so much so that his hands became deformed and he was unable to hold a brush.

One night, seeing his sacrificing friend at prayer, Dürer took his brush and immortalized those gnarled, unselfish hands on canvas. I had written this story in verse and had presented it at a church conference, where it was well received. But until Aladdin used it, only a handful had heard it.

Soon it was one of Gibson's most widely sought poems with sales that eventually reached the millions.

THE PRAYING HANDS

The *"Praying Hands"* are much, much more
than just a work of art,
They are the "soul's creation"
of a deeply thankful heart—
They are a *Priceless Masterpiece*
that love alone could paint,
And they reveal the selflessness
of an unheralded saint—
These hands so scarred and toilworn,
tell the story of a man
Who sacrificed his talent
in accordance with God's Plan—
For in God's Plan are many things
man cannot understand,
But we must trust God's judgment
and be guided by His Hand—
Sometimes He asks us to give up
our dreams of happiness,
Sometimes we must forego our hopes
of fortune and success—
Not all of us can triumph
or rise to heights of fame,
And many times *What Should Be Ours*,
goes to *Another Name*—
But he who makes a sacrifice,
so another may succeed,
Is indeed a true disciple
of our blessed Saviour's creed—
For when we "give ourselves away"
in sacrifice and love,

We are "laying up rich treasures"
in God's kingdom up above—
And hidden in gnarled, toilworn hands
is the truest *Art of Living*,
Achieved alone by those who've learned
the *"Victory of Giving"*—
For any sacrifice on earth,
made in the dear Lord's name,
Assures the giver of a place
in *Heaven's Hall of Fame*—
And who can say with certainty
Where the Greatest Talent Lies,
Or Who Will Be the Greatest
In Our Heavenly Father's Eyes!

But Aladdin wasn't finished. After "Praying Hands," he used a tribute I'd written to John Glenn's mother, following the astronaut's historic flight. It went like this:

When John was just a little boy,
You always found your greatest joy
In watching him from day to day
Exploring "new worlds" in his play . . .
For with a kite string in his hand
He soared into an unknown land,
And with uplifted childish eyes
He tried to penetrate the skies . . .
For little hands and minds reach out
To learn what life is all about,
And God in wisdom and in love
Directs His children's eyes above,
And it was with Our Father's grace
That your boy winged his way through space
And then came safely back to tell—
On earth and sea and sky, as well,
God's handiwork is everywhere
And heaven and earth alike declare
The glory of the King of kings
Who gave man all these wondrous things . . .
And God just chose a man named Glenn
To bring New Faith to "faithless men,"
For in this day of automation
Man strives to win his own salvation—

God's Ways are something man forgot,
But it took this humble astronaut
To tell the world that faith and truth,
Learned from his parents in his youth,
Have been his shield and armor plate
And gave him strength to penetrate
The vast and wonderful "unknown"
Where all the glory of God is shown . . .
For God never lets His children go
Alone to realms they do not know,
And your son John accomplished more
Than "space programs" were aiming for . . .
He won not just the world's acclaim,
Its plaudits, praise and hero's fame,
But God looked down upon your son
And softly said . . . "Well done! Well done!"
And as the Mother of "the first man in space"
You, too, deserve an honored place—
So on this Mother's Day we cheer
Our choice for the Mother of the Year!

My last Welk recollection came on November 23, 1963, the day following John F. Kennedy's assassination. I was in Lorain visiting my sister.
There, I received a call from Lawrence Welk, who asked if I could write
something appropriate for their show, which would be filmed the next
day. I said I would try.

Overnight I wrote the following poem and read it over the phone to a
Welk assistant. It went like this:

A TRIBUTE TO J.F.K.

His gallant soul has but taken flight
  into 'the land where there is no night'
He is not dead,
  he has only gone on
Into a brighter
  and more wonderful dawn . . .
For his passion for justice
  among men of good will
No violence can silence,
  no bullet can still . . .
For his spirit lives on
  and, like the warm sun,
It will nourish the dreams
  that he had begun . . .

So this hour of sorrow
   is only God's will,
For the 'good in this man
   is living here still' . . .
Forgive our transgressions
   and revive us anew
So we may draw closer
   to each other and YOU . . .
For unless 'God is guard',
   John Kennedy said,
'We're standing unguarded'
   with dreams that are dead . . .

For a nation too proud
   to kneel down and pray
Will crumble to chaos
   and descend to decay . . .
So use 'WHAT HE GAVE'
   for a REDEDICATION
And make this once more
   a God-fearing nation—
A symbol of hope—and
   a standard for good
As we lead in the struggle
   for a 'NEW BROTHERHOOD'!

All of this time, my verses were being reproduced in increasing num-
bers and mail was streaming into my office at an unbelievable pace.
People with all sorts of requests and problems wrote me for help, and
because I believe God opened this door as a ministry, I've never turned
my back on any correspondent. As a result, He has put me in touch with
some of the most beautiful people in the world. For the most part they
aren't famous or unusual, just full of a desire to serve God with all their
hearts, minds, and souls. And because I count myself as one of them,
I've received tremendous inspiration and joy from the dear souls who
have written to tell me that we share a common spiritual bond.

With Don McNeill on ABC's popular "Breakfast Club Show" in 1961. *Below:* Autographing books gives me a chance to meet people.

In 1960 Aladdin of the "Lawrence Welk Show" read my poem "The Priceless Gift" on nationwide television, thus reaching millions of people with God's wonderful message of love.

Lawrence Welk asked me to write a poem about John F. Kennedy's assassination, which was read on his show.

"The lady must own a million hats," someone said. I don't have quite that many, but I do love them—all colors, all materials, all styles. On these and the following pages you'll find pictures taken over the years of some of my favorite hats.

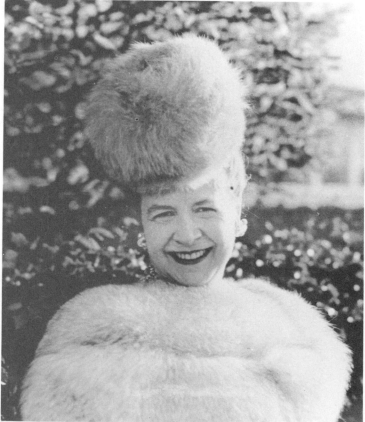

Part III:
The Later Years

19 *The Blessings That Followed*

HOW IT ALL HAPPENED

Six years ago on "The Lawrence Welk Show"
An artist who so many folks know
Received a card with a Christmas verse
That spoke of the Holy Christ Child's Birth—
And for some reason it caught his eye,
And I doubt today that he even knows Why.
For the reader and writer had never met
But the writer is one who will never forget
The joyous amazement and rapt surprise
When out of the starlit Christmas skies
Across the country from shore to shore
An unknown verse never heard before
Was heard by millions of listening ears,
And the writer's dream of many years
Was answered by God in a wonderful way,
And from that night to this present day
Aladdin still reads with his magic touch
The verses that people have liked so much—
And while it may look like a happenstance,
Or something born of a lucky chance,
The writer is sure that God drew the plan
And put it into the hands of man.
And, Aladdin,
   one of the Lawrence Welk band,
Just carried out what the Lord had planned
For I had prayed for many long years
Through disappointments and often tears
To find, without attempts to preach,
A way that I could somehow reach
Responsive hearts . . . much like my own
And tell them "No One Walks Alone"—
But little did I guess or know
My prayer would be answered on
   "The Lawrence Welk Show,"

For since "The Priceless Gift" was aired,
Through Aladdin's voice I've often shared
All the verses between these covers.
And through the years there may be others
That I can share with folks like you
For there's nothing I would rather do—
And this is the story of "How It Began"
Six years ago with "The Music Man."

*T*he poem above, written in 1966, tells the story of how my verses came to the attention of the American public. And the world. Because of the Welk program, which is seen in many foreign countries, John and Anna Steiner's elder daughter, Helen, of Lorain, Ohio, has gotten to speak to millions about her faith.

One of the results of the Welk exposure was a greatly increased demand for my verses. And because the free-enterprise system exists on the economic principle of supply and demand, more and more of my poems were published. The number of greeting cards bearing my name rose several thousandfold; still, people wrote to say they couldn't find them in their town. And when book publishers began printing my poems, people who frequent bookstores wrote to complain that they couldn't find this title or that title in their store.

Doubleday was the first to publish my poems in a hardcover book. That was in 1967, when they issued *Just For You*. It has sold hundreds of thousands of copies, and still is selling. Fleming H. Revell Company followed with several small books such as *Heart Gifts* and *Lovingly* before publishing three large-format books: *Someone Cares, Loving Promises* and *Somebody Loves You*. Together, these have sold in the millions. Subsequently, my verses have appeared on wall plaques, samplers, calendars, vases, and who knows what else!

All of which may sound very commercial and would be embarrassing—if I were garnering royalties on all those products. The truth is that I have not been made rich by the sales of my verses. Though I receive royalties from my books, I have managed to give away almost everything the Internal Revenue Service hasn't taken.

That's not to say I resent paying my fair share of the freight for the privilege of living in a democracy, yet I do sometimes get annoyed with all the paperwork involved in paying taxes.

Once I shared this frustration with our district director:

Taxes are something I "ungladly" pay
For there must be a more simple way
To figure out a tax return

On wages that you slave to earn
But I guess if taxes were easy to do
There'd be no jobs for folks like you
And I am glad there is some place to go
Where there are competent people who know
How to decipher this miserable mess
And accurately (I hope), correctly assess
What I should pay at the end of the year
For the special privilege of living here
But believe it or not, Mrs. Helen S. Rice
Does not object to the government's price.
It's just that unfathomable 1040 form
That creates in me an emotional storm!

The point is that I believe my poems are thoughts given me by God. I've only put some olden, golden truths to rhyme. So I don't think I should claim credit for the inspiration of someone else. Also, I don't write for the money. I never have nor will I ever. I write for the glory of God. If one person is helped or guided or inspired by something I've set to rhyme, then I'm repaid with love—something money can never equal.

20 *When We Let Go and Let God*

THE GOLDEN CHAIN OF FRIENDSHIP

FRIENDSHIP is a GOLDEN CHAIN,
The links are friends so dear,
And like a rare and precious jewel
It's treasured more each year . . .
It's clasped together firmly
With a love that's deep and true,
And it's rich with happy memories
And fond recollections, too . . .
Time can't destroy its beauty
For, as long as memory lives,
Years can't erase the pleasure
That the joy of friendship gives . . .
For friendship is a priceless gift
That can't be bought or sold,
But to have an understanding friend
Is worth far more than gold . . .
And the GOLDEN CHAIN of FRIENDSHIP
Is a strong and blessed tie
Binding kindred hearts together
As the years go passing by.

*H*as public recognition changed me? I think not, the reason being that I received plenty of adulation as a young woman when I began speaking all over the country in the 1920s. Early in my life I saw the shallowness of the celebrity image.

Being treated as special and unique may be some people's cup of tea, but it has never been mine, because, frankly, I've never felt that unique. Furthermore, prima donnas are big bores and after their moment in the sun most end up feeling depressed and bitter.

From the beginning, I've longed for permanence. I suspect it is in my genes. People with whom I grew up didn't cotton to those who were phonies or thought more of themselves than they should have.

I've always sought things of substance—lasting things—which is why I count my faith the most important thing in my life. Following my love of God is my love of the friends who provide life with depth and meaning.

Nothing that has come from whatever fame I've achieved in the last twenty years has given me more satisfaction than the people who have come into my life as a result of that "fame."

Thousands, no, *tens* of thousands have told me in person, called, or written me to say how much they have received from my writings.

What they don't realize is that the greatest thrill I receive is learning about their appreciation. That is because every time someone tells me that my words have given them strength or guidance or inspiration, I realize God has opened another door for me, and I thank Him each time for the privilege of being a small part of His plan.

Nothing could be clearer than that all of the things that have happened to me are part of a divine plan. The events are too preposterous for me to believe differently. Think of it. How could some person with my background, a woman without position or wealth or family name, a woman with only a high-school education, be given the role in life that I have received? The only answer I have ever been able to find is that I have been a willing servant, and God uses willing disciples in fantastic ways. The Bible tells us what happened to Peter and Andrew when they left their nets and followed Christ. Exciting things always happen to anyone who is willing to follow Him without reservations.

Next I want to tell you about a few of the special people whom God has sent into my life. Perhaps quoting from some of their letters will show you how they have inspired me.

21 *Pen Pals*

THE HOUSE OF FRIENDSHIP

You are my friend—
This is the House of Friendship—
As my guest, will you partake of the joy
    of Friendship with me?
For, while you are here, Friendship is
    your genial host,
And the welcome that awaits you is from
    the heart . . .
When you go, may you not go alone,
But may you take with you the warmth and
    beauty of Friendship,
And may you bring it back each time you
    come to visit beneath this friendly roof.

*G*od has once again made me aware in the middle of a very hot, very busy season when all is work, hurry, confusion, and earthly frustration that we must quiet ourselves and our minds for the sake of our very physical existence.

"Last evening, as night approached, I thought of you, Mrs. Rice, and your need for physical healing. I wanted to share with you the warm wind that carried the smell of new-mown hay and the sound of tree toads and whippoorwills. It is in such simple, yet beautiful things that we are given a healing peace that could only come from a loving God."

From a professional author? No, from a good friend and regular correspondent. The woman is unbelievably wise and full of insight about spiritual things and life and nature, and she is a constant source of inspiration to me.

A favorite correspondent of mine comes from Hamilton, Ontario. Her name is Mother (Hilda May) Price. She is ninety-five years young at this writing. I am her "adopted" daughter. Mrs. Price is the mother of a son, but she never had a daughter of her own.

Several years ago, she wrote to tell me of her appreciation of my poems. I responded and thus began a loving friendship. She told me that she wished I were her daughter, and I said that since my mother and father had gone to heaven, I needed an earthly parent and would be honored to have her as a proxy. Ever since, she has signed her letters MOTHER PRICE and I, "your loving daughter, HELEN."

Another wonderful pen pal of mine is Kathleen Mimms of Newport, Kentucky. Kathleen first wrote me several years ago after she had read "The End of the Road Is But a Bend in the Road." Undergoing great tribulation at the time, the poem seemed, she told me, to be providentially sent. The words leaped into her heart and whereas she had felt desperately alone, she suddenly felt God nearer than ever before.

As a result, Kathleen has grown in spiritual strength and become a beacon of light to many others who have faced difficulties and defeat. She certainly has been a light of inspiration to me.

Whenever I am feeling low or defeated, I can always get a lift from the day's mail. From people who may be small in the world's eyes, but are spiritual giants in God's sight, I draw power to tackle my problems and go on. There are so many I could name—Janie Bell from Greenwich, Connecticut, and Frances Helms of Elgin, Iowa, are two who come quickly to mind.

Of course, when the load gets too heavy for my fabulous secretary, Mary Jo Eling, and me, I have to find a short cut in order to see that everyone is answered. Recently, this response went out to hundreds who had sent me Easter greetings:

I won't try to express what my heart feels today . . . for there are no words in which I could say . . . all that is tearing my heart apart . . . for there'd be no place to begin to start . . . I only know I am "lost in a sea" . . . of unanswered letters addressed to me . . . and daily I watch this "mountain grow steeper" . . . and hour by hour "my sadness grows deeper" . . . for you've all become part of my poems . . . and a part of myself lives in all of your homes . . . but my days are so crowded and my hours are so few . . . and my strength and endurance is waning, too . . . so when I don't write, do not be dismayed . . . for my memories of you are the kind that don't fade . . . and remember in reading these poems of mine . . . I am talking to you in each God-filled line . . . for you're part of my life and part of my heart . . . and through God we are only a prayer apart . . . and I can only thank God and trust Him to relay . . . all that I feel in my heart but can't say!

My life has been filled with fountains of blessings in the form of letters from all parts of the earth. From these letters that continue to come in, it seems so many people are identifying with me and finding meaning in my poems. Actually, I am talking to them from my heart in these poems, and many of my verses are "woven" from "the silken strands of thought" that have come to me while I was talking with people or reading their letters.

It is impossible to read through my daily mail and be untouched by the tragic things that happen in the lives of people all over this world. Often we try to push these unhappy things away from us so that our lives are not too darkened by the shadows all around us. But we know in our hearts that life is trouble and trouble is life and that in our "journey to eternity" we experience many heartaches and our cross becomes increasingly difficult to carry.

I have to content myself in knowing the same God who abides in me abides in them and, through Him, we can communicate without speaking a word . . . for, when Heart speaks to Heart, time and space mean little, and when kindred minds meet, physical limitations fade before the power of Spiritual Reality. I feel we have complete identification because we are "joint heirs" to the Love of God, which is beyond all explaining or comprehending. We meet God in Spirit and through Him, we meet each other. And the Spirit is much greater than life itself and bigger than feeble, little words that a human mind could express.

I truly do believe that the loving interest in my works did not come by chance or happenstance but by "Divine Design," and I know that all these things I say are just timeless truths that are constantly repeated through the ages. Again I am reminded of the majestic truth of Ecclesiastes, for "there is nothing new" and "what has been will be" (*see* 1:8–11).

Over and over, the words of God's wisdom are echoed down through the ages, and the little things I write were long ago expressed on ancient, ageless pages.

22 *They Keep Me Going*

PRAYERS ARE THE STAIRS TO GOD

Prayers are the stairs
We must climb every day,
If we would reach God
There is no other way,
For we learn to know God
When we meet Him in prayer
And ask Him to lighten
Our burden of care—
So start in the morning
And, though the way's steep,
Climb ever upward
'Til your eyes close in sleep—
For prayers are the stairs
That lead to the Lord,
And to meet Him in prayer
Is the climber's reward.

*T*hough I enjoy hearing from old friends who write at fairly regular intervals, the preponderance of my mail is from people who have just come in contact with some verse I've written. Often the poem has reached them in a moment of trial or despair.

The letters that I receive have proven over and over, again and again, that the love and mercy of Jesus Christ is no ethereal story. It is truly the rapture and the glory that comes to those who believe beyond all believing! To have shared the inner experience of many human beings is a privilege accorded to few people. I have seen them stand firm, strong, and undaunted under all circumstances, and they all have qualities of saints!

When my need is inspiration, letters that I have received are there to fulfill it. I have kept excerpts from a great many letters, but I actually think I have so many treasured memories in my heart, it would not be really necessary to keep my files!

Let me give you a few examples. A woman from the Midwest wrote:

When I was nine, I had an operation for a brain tumor. After the operation, the doctor told my parents that I wouldn't have very long to live, but my mother put all her trust and faith in God that He would spare my life. Through the help and loving care of God, also that of my mother, and cards and prayers which I received from some wonderful people I knew, I'm living today. I know now that without God beside me I would never have pulled through.

When I came home from the hospital, I was completely blind. But as weeks went by, I slowly started regaining part of my sight, which according to the doctors was impossible. After a while, I regained part of my vision in one eye. Although I'm still handicapped in my right arm and leg from the operation, I thank God for what He has given me.

Often people who have found a blessing in one of my poems write to ask what I need or what they can do for me. I usually answer that they already have made my day by taking time to drop me a line.

Once a Catholic sister named Sister Mary Felicitas wrote that she wished there was something she could do to repay me for my poems. When I showed the letter to Mary Jo Eling, my faithful secretary for the last twelve years, she said, "Oh, Sister Mary Felicitas was one of my high-school teachers."

"Well, in that case," I said, "Sister Mary already has repaid me by sending you to help," and that's what I told her in my letter.

From the friend of a bereaved mother:

Words cannot adequately tell what your poem "When I Must Leave You" has meant to a very dear friend of mine. Recently, this lady lost her teenage son in an accident. Priests, ministers and all who love her reached out in comfort and concern. I know how inadequate and empty I felt in an attempt to help. Then we discovered your poem. Believe me, it has meant more than any other single thing. She has several copies of it, has memorized it and lives it.

And another:

I am a teacher. Every day before we begin class, I read one of your poems. In last year's class, one girl had a very poor attitude, but your verses helped change it. She became one of the sweetest girls in the class, and since graduation she has written me three letters thanking me for changing her outlook. Also, you'll never know how many true and lasting friends I've made through our mutual interest in your writings.

Naturally, I am pleased to hear such words of praise, but I keep reminding such correspondents that . . .

> Nothing that I think or write is mine and
>   mine alone,
> So if you found some beauty in any word or
>   line,
> It's just "your soul's reflection" in
>   proximity with mine.

Few letters are more inspiring than this one, from a girl named Deborah Reker of Fort Thomas, Kentucky. She overcame great adversity through the application of her faith in God. She wrote me recently:

In 1967, I was a 17-year-old senior with an *A* average in school, and a Kentucky tennis champion whose future was bright and promising. Then I was involved in a serious auto accident. I was told by doctors that it was unlikely I would ever walk again. But I refused to believe them. Since 1967, I have had 42 operations on my right knee and hip. Several times, doctors suggested the leg be amputated, but I refused, praying and re-reading your beautiful poems from which I drew strength to go on.

During my illness and between operations, I was a premed student at the University of Cincinnati on a full scholarship and working as a nurse's aide to help supplement my mother's earnings. My father died a year before my accident and Mother had to go to work.

Today I am a registered nurse and a tennis pro, too. I still have my leg, although it's not very pretty and I walk with a limp. Pain is my constant companion, but your poetry, Mother's never-ending support, and my faith are more effective than any pain medication . . . . I've learned to follow the saying "When you reach the end of your rope, tie a knot in it and hang on." Thanks so much for bringing encouragement and hope into my life and the lives of countless others like me!

God bless *you,* Deborah. Your life speaks more eloquently about God's love and mercy than any poem that has ever been written.

23 *My Outlook on Life*

LET NOT YOUR HEART BE TROUBLED

Whenever I am troubled
      and lost in deep despair
I bundle all my troubles up
      and go to God in prayer . . .
I tell Him I am heartsick
      and lost and lonely, too,
That my mind is deeply burdened
      and I don't know what to do . . .
But I know He stilled the tempest
      and calmed the angry sea
And I humbly ask if in His love
      He'll do the same for me . . .
And then I just keep *Quiet*
      and think only thoughts of *Peace*
And if I abide in *Stillness*
      my "restless murmurings" cease.

*B*ecause so many people write and ask me about my opinion on various problems and matters of faith, and because I find it so hard to answer each individual personally, I am going to devote the rest of these pages to those most-raised questions. I don't for one minute think that I have any new insights into the age-old issues that have always troubled mankind, but if I can help some travel-weary pilgrim with my statements of faith, I am willing to make them.

I am a very simple, uncomplicated person, and "a child's faith" is all I possess. There is nothing I need to know, or even try to understand, if I place myself completely in God's great and mighty Hand!

I do believe in miracles. I do believe in prayer. I believe completely and without reservation in God. I believe I am a small, struggling sinner, but this does not trouble me too much. I know that if I ask God to forgive me, He will; and I know that He died for me, so who am I to ask Him to explain how His plan will work?

I know that God is the Answer to everything. I do not believe anything ever dies, for in the Kingdom of the Lord there is nothing lost forever—not a grain of sand, not a drop of rain, not a crystal of dew. So

108

why would we ever think that God would create man to end in nothing-ness? I solve my problems one by one, asking nothing of tomorrow—only God's will be done.

I have no formula but faith, no Gospel but God, no creed but Christ, and no love but the Lord. And there could be no joy without Jesus!

While none of us knows what the future holds, we all can know the One who holds our future. With that knowledge we can climb the hills ahead and scan the mountain peaks. And no road is too rough and no hill is too high, if we walk in the light of the Lord, for with God on our side, who can be against us! We win not on our own strength or valor, or with our own talent, knowledge, or skill, but we win the battle of life when we have complete confidence in God.

What happens to you in the years that lie ahead is not as important as *how* you take what happens to you. And the real secret of happiness is not in doing what one likes but in liking what one has to do. All real knowledge is gained along the pathway of experience, and how much you *get* depends on how much you *give*.

The way to real growth is not to become more powerful or more wealthy or more famous but to become more human and more tolerant. Gold has no value, unless it is reminted into goodness.

Before we can master life, we must first learn self-mastery. And high principles and moral strength are only acquired through an uphill strug-gle to maintain integrity, honor, and reliability. Remember "Ideals Are Like Stars." We cannot reach them, but like the mariner at sea, we can always look skyward and chart our course by them.

> In this world of casual carelessness
> > it's discouraging to try
> To keep our morals and standards
> > and our *Ideals High* . . .
> We are ridiculed and laughed at
> > by the smart sophisticate
> Who proclaims in brittle banter
> > that such things are out of date . . .
> But no life is worth the living
> > unless it's built on truth,
> And we lay our life's foundation
> > in the golden years of youth . . .
> So allow no one to stop you
> > or hinder you from laying
> A firm and strong foundation
> > made of *Faith and Love and Praying* . . .
> And remember that *Ideals*
> > are like *Stars Up In The Sky*,

You can never really reach them,
      hanging in heavens high . . .
But like the mighty mariner
      who sailed the storm-tossed sea,
And used the *Stars To Chart His Course*
      with skill and certainty,
You too can *Chart Your Course in Life*
      with High Ideals and Love,
For *High Ideals are like the Stars*
      that light the sky above . . .
You cannot ever reach them,
      but Lift Your Heart Up High
And your *Life* will be as *Shining*
      as the *Stars Up In The Sky.*

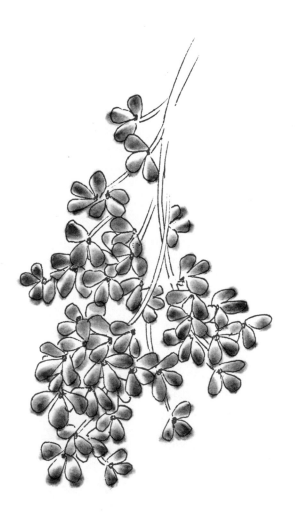

24 Never Give Up

THE SEASONS OF THE SOUL

Why am I cast down
            and despondently sad
When I long to be happy
            and joyous and glad?
Why is my heart heavy
            with unfathomable weight
As I try to escape
            this soul-saddened state?
I ask myself often—
            "What makes life this way,
Why is the song silenced
            in the heart that was gay?"
And then with God's help
            it all becomes clear.
The *Soul* has its *Seasons*
            just the same as the year—
I too must pass through
            life's autumn of dying,
A desolate period
            of heart-hurt and crying,
Followed by winter
            in whose frostbitten hand
My heart is as frozen
            as the snow-covered land—
Yes, man too must pass
            through the seasons God sends,
Content in the knowledge
            that everything ends,
And oh what a blessing
            to know there are reasons
And to find that our soul
            must, too, have its seasons—
Bounteous Seasons
            and *Barren Ones*, too,
Times for rejoicing
            and times to be blue,

But meeting these seasons
        of dark desolation
With strength that is born
        of anticipation
That comes from knowing
            that "autumn-time sadness"
Will surely be followed
            by a "Springtime of Gladness."

*Y*ou may be facing some dark hours right now and the clouds of despair at times seem to threaten to close out the light that shines so brightly from your eternal soul. But don't let this happen, for you must remember that dark hours come into the lives of us all.

Our greatest comfort is to know that "the same God who helped us before is ready and willing to help us once more." All God asks of us is that we believe, and we must believe enough and have enough faith in Him that we will refuse to let anything shut Him out of our lives . . . .

There are many times when I am ready to give up—but I know that all I have to do is go to God in prayer! I know this is true of everyone and I often pray:

Oh, Blessed Father, hear this prayer . . . and keep all of us in Your care . . . give us patience and inner sight, too . . . just as You often used to do . . . when on the shores of The Galilee . . . You touched the blind and they could see . . . and cured the man who long was lame . . . when he but called Your Holy Name!

You Are So Great . . . we are so small . . . and when trouble comes . . . as it does to us all . . . there's so little that we can do . . . except to place our trust in You!

So, take the Saviour's loving Hand . . . and do not try to understand . . . just let Him lead you where He will . . . through "pastures green and waters still" . . . and place yourself in His loving care . . . and He will gladly help you bear . . . whatever lies ahead of you . . . and God will see you safely through . . . and no earthly pain is ever too much . . . if God bestows His merciful touch.

So, I commend you into His care . . . with a loving thought and a Special Prayer . . . and always remember, Whatever Betide You . . . God is always beside you . . . and you cannot go beyond His love and care . . . for we are all a Part of God, and God is everywhere!

While God will not instantly turn our dark hours into sunshine, He will give us the strength to walk on in the darkest despair, until we reach a brighter tomorrow! Of course, you know we cannot do this on our own. But all the things that we can't do, God can!

Never begin a day without first putting your life in God's Hands and looking into His face and asking for strength and guidance through the day. So, start each day by saying, "Good Morning, God," and always remember . . .

> Life is a mixture
> of sunshine and rain,
> Laughter and teardrops,
> Pleasure and pain—
> Low tides and high tides,
> Mountains and plains,
> Triumphs, defeats,
> and losses and gains—
> But there never was a cloud
> That the SUN didn't SHINE THROUGH
> And there's nothing that's IMPOSSIBLE
> For Jesus Christ to do!

25 *With His Help You Can Carry Your Cross*

BRIGHTEN THE CORNER WHERE YOU ARE

We cannot all be famous or be listed in "WHO'S WHO,"
But every person great or small has important work to do,
For seldom do we realize the importance of small deeds
Or to what degree of greatness unnoticed kindness leads—
For it's not the big celebrity in a world of fame and praise,
But it's doing unpretentiously in undistinguished ways
The work that God assigned to us, unimportant as it seems,
That makes our task outstanding and brings reality to dreams—
So do not sit and idly wish for wider, new dimensions
Where you can put in practice your many "GOOD INTENTIONS"—
But at the spot God placed you begin at once to do
Little things to brighten up the lives surrounding you,
For if everybody brightened up the spot on which they're standing
By being more considerate and a little less demanding,
This dark old world would very soon eclipse the "EVENING STAR"
If everybody BRIGHTENED UP THE CORNER WHERE THEY ARE!

Some people go around underestimating their great potential. You are a very special person, and you should thank God every day that you have a keen, sensitive, and perceptive mind. God has made you a beautiful, warm, wonderful individual.

You are a child of God, and you are beautiful inside. If you only give it a chance, this spiritual beauty will shine through and it will draw other people to you like a magnet.

Now, we all experience some "dark nights of the soul," and no one can go through life without experiencing them. I have come face-to-face with them many times in my long life, and I have often tangled with them on "Life's Highway to Heaven."

I know in our modern society we are led to believe that we can in some way free ourselves completely from these troublesome feelings, if we practice "the right methods." But this is not so, for life consists of carry-

114

ing our crosses. And if we learn to do this, we can turn our crosses into crowns!

Remember, our "crosses" assume many different shapes. Sometimes we have to content ourselves in a narrow sphere, when we feel we have capacities for much higher work, and often we have to show a smiling face, when our hearts are breaking inside.

Nobody finds carrying a cross easy to bear, and we never seek them out of our own accord. But when we do "pick up our cross and carry it," then we grow in grace and we grow closer to God and to one another.

Just "brighten the corner where you are" and realize that you, too, are filling a very important place.

Don't dwell on your shortcomings. Focus all your attention on others, and you will find, in giving your love and attention to others, you, too, will be enriched.

Recently I have been going through many hours of soul searching and walking through dark times that come to us all. But I know God is behind the "dark cloud" that engulfs me, and I must endure it until He removes the darkness, for this is not a destructive experience but a constructive one. I am sure He is trying to awaken me to a new awareness of how to best serve Him. And after my old self dies completely, I will have moved a little closer to God.

Each day I become more aware that all these things I am experiencing have been felt by others down through the centuries, and never has it been so vivid to me as when I read Psalm 102. I can hear myself saying these same words, asking God to hear my prayer and not to hide His face, and I, too, feel that "my days vanish like smoke" (*see* verse 3) and my heart is stricken. So, in reading through passages in the Bible, I realize this is God and that He is trying once more to "Take Me and Break Me and Make Me Just What He Wants Me to Be."

> Take me and break me and make me, dear God
> Just what You want me to be—
> Give me the strength to accept what You send
> And eyes with the vision to see
> All the small arrogant ways that I have
> And the vain little things that I do
> Make me aware that I'm often concerned
> More with myself than with You.
> Uncover before me my weakness and greed
> And help me to search deep inside
> So I may discover how easy it is
> To be selfishly lost in my pride—
> And then in Thy goodness and mercy
> Look down on this weak, erring one

And tell me that I am forgiven
For all I've so willfully done,
And teach me to humbly start following
The path that the dear Saviour trod
So I'll find at the end of life's journey
"A HOME IN THE CITY OF GOD."

26 Go To Your Bible for Help

THERE'S PEACE AND CALM IN THE 23RD PSALM

With THE LORD as "YOUR SHEPHERD"
    you have all that you need,
For, if you "FOLLOW IN HIS FOOTSTEPS"
    wherever HE may lead,
HE will guard and guide and keep you
    in HIS loving, watchful care
And, when traveling in "dark valleys,"
    "YOUR SHEPHERD" will be there . . .
HIS goodness is unfailing,
    HIS kindness knows no end,
For THE LORD is a "GOOD SHEPHERD"
    on whom you can depend . . .
So when your heart is troubled,
    you'll find quiet, peace and calm
If you open up the Bible
    and just read this treasured Psalm.

My prescription for you right now is one that a noted preacher once recommended. And it never fails to work, if it is followed precisely and without fail.

When you awaken, read the Twenty-third Psalm. Do not recite it from memory. Read it very slowly and very carefully and with deep meditation.

Do not read it hurriedly, but think about each word and phrase and let your mind soak up the wonderful assurance that there is in these words. Most of us know this psalm by heart, but we repeat it without ever realizing the great and full meaning of it. It is the most powerful piece of writing in this world!

Just think what it means to know that the Lord is *your* Shepherd and that He is leading you and anointing your scars and heart-hurt with the balm of His love. The more you think about this, the more you become aware of its power. You can heal your body and mind and heart with

117

this psalm. God promises to restore your soul, revive your weary body, take you into a cool, clear place where you can rest and, no matter how steep the hill or mountain is, the Lord is going to climb it with you.

Just writing this has already given me strength. The sheep are never afraid, because they know the Shepherd will lead them into green pastures, beside the still waters. And so, as you come to "dark places" in your life, just reach out for the Hand of the Shepherd. If you stop and get very quiet and still, you will feel the Presence of God.

I often say this when I am troubled, and I imagine I am just a "little lamb" who doesn't know where to go, and that I have no one to follow but the Shepherd. I know the Shepherd will not let me fall over the precipice. He will not let me drink in the swift water, for I might slip and fall in. And I know that no matter what happens, He will go with me, even through "the Valley of the Shadows." With that knowledge, what is there to fear?

He will bring you safely through, no matter which "side of life or death" is your destination. You cannot lose, for He brings His children safely through everything!

Just read this treasured psalm every day, and you will be surprised how calm and wonderful you feel.

27 You Can Really Turn Defeat Into Victory

YESTERDAY, TODAY, AND TOMORROW!

Yesterday's dead,
Tomorrow's unborn,
So there's nothing to fear
And nothing to mourn,
For all that is past
And all that has been
Can never return
To be lived once again—
And what lies ahead
Or the things that will be
Are still in GOD'S HANDS
So it is not up to me
To live in the future
That is God's great unknown,
For the past and the present
God claims for His own.
So all I need do
Is to live for TODAY
And trust God to show me
THE TRUTH and THE WAY—
For it's only the memory
Of things that have been
And expecting tomorrow
To bring trouble again
That fills my today,
Which God wants to bless,
With uncertain fears
And borrowed distress—
For all I need live for
Is this one little minute,
For life's HERE and NOW
And ETERNITY'S in it.

*W*hile we all wonder why bad things have to happen to "good people," we also know that just being good and loving God and trying to serve Him does not guarantee us immunity from trouble, suffering, pain, and sickness. But we must remember that "God knows best"! And we can be sure that, while it is impossible for us to understand *why* things happen as they do, there is always a definite purpose behind everything that happens to us, even though we may take long months or years to discover what the true purpose was.

It is always comforting to know that "the more we endure with patience and grace, the stronger we grow and the more we can face." And what a reassurance it is to know that God will never, never, never forsake us.

We must learn to keep our courageous spirits strong and unconquerable, for you know there is nothing that is really a limitation, if we see it through God's Eyes! Many times physically whole people are very crippled spiritually. And while it is a blessing to have a strong body free from all pain and suffering, it is much better to have a strong spirit that can accept and endure what God sends, and keep growing in soul stature with each new affliction.

My poem called "Yesterday, Today, and Tomorrow" has brought much comment from people who have received insight from it. To know there is no tomorrow, no yesterday but only the minute you are living in (and that minute has eternity in it) makes it possible to *accept* the things that are happening to you.

There is a Divine Mystery in suffering and a strange and supernatural power in it which has never been fathomed by human reasoning. But it seems that no one attains a real, closer relationship with God, unless they travel the hill called Calvary.

We know that grapes must be crushed before there is wine to drink, and wheat must be bruised in order that it be made into bread to feed a hungry world. Unbroken and unbruised men and women are of little use in life, for we can never truly "dry another's tears" or share their sorrow unless we have wept ourselves and experienced our own Gethsemane.

One of my favorite stories is about the young man who went to an aged saint and asked him to pray that he might become more patient. So the good saint started to pray, and he said, "Send this young man tribulation; send it morning, noon, and night." And the young man interrupted and said, "No! No! I want *patience,* not *tribulation!*" But the old saint said, "It is only tribulation that worketh patience." So if you would be patient, you must first have tribulation.

Somehow I share your sorrow and your problems, for I know problems come to us all. But God does not promise us security *from* the storm, only security *in* the storm. Life is not a "flower-strewn path" but a "rocky road," so it is not for us to seek an "easy passage" but await a "safe landing"!

I know in my heart that if we want to travel "the Highway to Heaven," we will constantly be in need of greater depths of experience. No one can "swim on the top of water" if "the Waters of Woe" are only ankle deep. And remember, *God never gives us more than we can handle.*

God never said *die not, sorrow not,* or *suffer not,* but He did say, "Fear not!" And when you take the fear out of the "rough trials of life," then all the terrible experiences become understandable, and all the terrible experiences become understandable, and all the trials and sufferings of life become bearable.

In my own personal experiences, I can truly say that what I once believed was a satisfying relationship with God has "opened up like a flower in the sun"! I find now that I never really knew the "true wonder of God," for I know it is impossible to comprehend His greatness. So while things have not been very well with me physically, I can truthfully say, "All is well with my soul!"

And best of all, I know now that none of us can survive on the knowledge borrowed from the troubles others have. We have to make it on our own, for only through enduring excruciating experiences can we ever acquire the spiritual knowledge that lifts us completely above our earthly tribulations.

Paradoxical though it is, there is nothing in life worthwhile that is not attained through conflict. The people who have never suffered nor had deep sorrow are unaware how lacking in spiritual strength they are, for they have never built up anything within them to withstand the shock of sorrow and trouble.

Last year I spent a long time in the hospital, and while I am now coming back to my office for a few hours each day when it is possible, it is still very difficult to get adjusted to my new, limited life-style, for it is much more difficult than I ever expected.

I am so aware that there is so much to do in God's vineyard and so little time to do it in. But I'm sure God is restraining me for a purpose, and He never makes mistakes. I think it is God's will that sometimes our minds seem frozen and life stands still . . . and there comes a time we must slacken our pace and accept the fact "we can't run every race"!

Then, too, I think God only takes away our comforts and privileges to make us better Christians, and I personally know that I could never have known God nor loved Him as much without this soul-enlightening

touch! Each limitation brings me closer to the greatness and the goodness of God.

I really never knew what tears were, until I had shed some myself, for
how can we tell when people's hearts are crying, when our hearts have
never wept? And it is so true that the greatest gifts we can give to one
another are the gifts of love and understanding.

28 *Parting From Loved Ones*

THE LEGEND OF THE RAINDROP

The legend of the raindrop
      Has a lesson for us all
As it trembled in the heavens
      Questioning whether it should fall—
For the glistening raindrop argued
      To the genie of the sky,
"I am beautiful and lovely
      As I sparkle here on high,
And hanging here I will become
      Part of the rainbow's hue
And I'll shimmer like a diamond
      For all the world to view" . . .
But the genie told the raindrop,
      "Do not hesitate to go,
For you will be more beautiful
      If you fall to earth below,
For you will sink into the soil
      And be lost a while from sight,
But when you reappear on earth,
      You'll be looked on with delight;
For you will be the raindrop
      That quenched the thirsty ground
And helped the lovely flowers
      To blossom all around,
And in your resurrection
      You'll appear in queenly clothes
With the beauty of the lily
      And the fragrance of the rose;
Then, when you wilt and wither,
      You'll become part of the earth
And make the soil more fertile
      And give new flowers birth" . . .
For there is nothing ever lost
      Or *Eternally Neglected,*

For *Everything God Ever Made*
Is Always Resurrected;
So trust God's all-wise wisdom
And doubt the Father never,
For in *His Heavenly Kingdom*
There Is Nothing Lost Forever.

*D*eath is just as it should be—we are and then we are not. It is like the blowing out of a lamp or the closing of a door. If we did not go to sleep, we could never know the joy of awakening. And if we did not die, we could not live eternally.

I know in my heart that God will take care of those who lose a loved one and give them strength to meet each day as it comes, for no one on earth has ever escaped the same emotions you may be feeling in your heart right now. So may God comfort you and show you the way. But remember, God does not comfort us to make us more comfortable. He comforts us so that we may also become comforters.

In my husband's tragic death, which was so hurried and unscheduled, it was difficult for me, when I was very young, to understand or accept it. But now I see that his sudden death transformed my entire life. I never could have done what I am doing now, if I had not felt the pangs of sorrow, for you cannot dry the tears of those who weep, unless you have cried yourself.

My father started on his journey into eternity when I was just eighteen. I know how bewildered and lost I was, and it took me many years to understand just why God took him from me when I needed him so much. But now that I have grown older, I have learned that God was giving me a "gift," and that gift was the chance to grow in grace and soul-stature.

We often wonder why God chooses the "darkness of sorrow" as a path to Him. But in the "dazzling light of the day" we cannot see beyond our own little world. Living in the sunshine, we become earthbound. But when the darkness comes, our eyes are forced heavenward. And when it gets too dark for us to see with our own eyes, then we must put our hand in the Hand of God and let Him lead the way. He is trying to teach us how to see in the "darkness" as well as in the "light."

When death comes, it sobers and saddens our hearts, for it still remains the impenetrable mystery. But none of us can escape parting from our loved ones, and it is on the "Wings of Death" that we "soar" a little closer to God and to each other.

Great Nature just opens up her arms and receives back the fleshy garments that clothe our loved ones' souls. And they rise unencumbered to meet God, and they wait for us in that place where there are no separations and time is not counted by years.

Of course, to me, death is just another step along the Pathway of Life, and it gives so much meaning and purpose to all living. It gives us the great joy of heading happily towards the ultimate goal of every Christian, and that is to live forever in the "Unending Sunshine of God's Love"!

I believe we just "burst our chrysalis of clay" and fare forth into new fields of usefulness. And just as God gives us our loved ones and does not lose them in giving, so we do not lose them in returning them to Him . . . for Life is Eternal, Love is Immortal, and Death is just a Horizon beyond which we cannot see with our narrow, earthly vision.

29 *The Summing Up*

"FLOWERS LEAVE THEIR FRAGRANCE ON THE HAND THAT BESTOWS THEM"

You can't do a kindness
    without a reward,
Not in silver or gold
    but in joy from the Lord—
You can't light a candle
    to show others the way
Without feeling the warmth
    of that bright little ray,
And you can't pluck a rose,
    all fragrant with dew,
Without part of its fragrance
    remaining with you.

*S*o now you know the truth of what I told you in the beginning: I am a very simple, uncomplicated person, just one of God's children, living under His daily care. I believe I am a lot like you. I have all your faults and all your shortcomings, and maybe some you don't have. I sin; I cry; I lose my way. That is why I begin each day with this prayer:

Bless me, Heavenly Father,
    forgive my erring ways,
Grant me strength to serve Thee,
    put purpose to my days . . .
Give me understanding
    enough to make me kind
So I may judge all people
    with my heart and not my mind . . .
And teach me to be patient
    in everything I do,
Content to trust *Your* Wisdom
    and to follow after *You* . . .
And help me when I falter
    and hear me when I pray
And receive me in *Thy Kingdom*
    to dwell with *Thee* some day.

My hope is that from the pages of this book you have learned something more than my life story. My purpose was to show how even the most unworthy "worker in the vineyard of the Lord" can receive His blessing. No one is more unworthy than I, and no one has been more blessed.

Whatever good, whatever help, whatever wisdom, whatever inspiration that may have come to you from these pages should be credited to the leading of His Holy Spirit, not my faltering pen:

> If you found any beauty
>   in the poems of this book
> Or some peace and some comfort
>   in a word or line,
> Don't give me praise
>   or wordly acclaim
> For the words that you read
>   are not mine . . .
> I borrowed them all
>   to share with you
> From our HEAVENLY FATHER
>   above,
> And the joy that you felt
>   was GOD speaking to you
> As HE flooded your heart
>   with HIS LOVE.

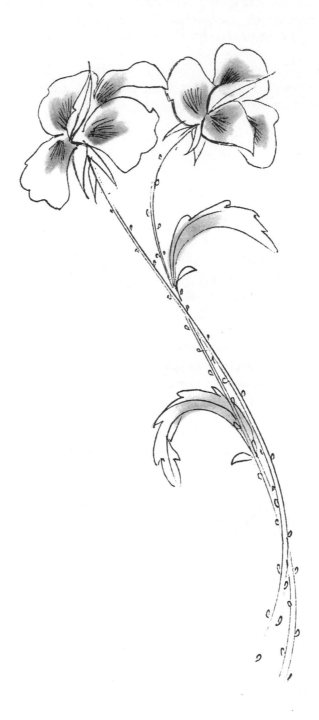